THE DARK SIDE OF BI

When Data Misleads Decision-Makers

NAKEL W. A. NIKIEMA

© **Copyright 2025 - All rights reserved.**

The content contained within this book may not be reproduced, duplicated or transmitted without direct written permission from the author or the publisher.

Under no circumstances will any blame or legal responsibility be held against the publisher, or author, for any damages, reparation, or monetary loss due to the information contained within this book, either directly or indirectly.

Legal Notice:

This book is copyright protected. It is only for personal use. You cannot amend, distribute, sell, use, quote or paraphrase any part, or the content within this book, without the consent of the author or publisher.

Disclaimer Notice:

Please note the information contained within this document is for educational and entertainment purposes only. All effort has been executed to present accurate, up to date, reliable, complete information. No warranties of any kind are declared or implied. Readers acknowledge that the author is not engaged in the rendering of legal, financial, medical or professional advice. The content within this book has been derived from various sources. Please consult a licensed professional before attempting any techniques outlined in this book.

By reading this document, the reader agrees that under no circumstances is the author responsible for any losses, direct or indirect, that are incurred as a result of the use of the information contained within this document, including, but not limited to, errors, omissions, or inaccuracies.

TABLE OF CONTENTS

Introduction   7

1. THE ILLUSION OF ACCURACY   15
   The Psychological Comfort of Precision   17
   The Role of Assumptions in Data Accuracy   20
   Why Context Is Everything   23
   The Effects of Blind Trust   25
   Final Thoughts   27

2. GARBAGE IN, GARBAGE OUT   31
   Data as a Reflection of Reality (Or Not)   33
   What Makes Data "Garbage" in the First Place?   34
   How Bad Data Gets Collected?   38
   The Hidden Danger of "Fixing" Data   40
   Why More Data Doesn't Mean Better Data   42
   Why GIGO Still Persists?   44
   Final Thoughts   47

3. CORRELATION VS. CAUSATION   49
   Definition of Correlation (And Its Limits)   51
   The Three Main Types of False Causation   53
   Distinguishing Correlation From Causation   57
   When Correlation Is Still Useful   60
   Final Thoughts   63

4. OVERFITTING AND FALSE PATTERNS   65
   What Is Overfitting?   66
   False Patterns: Seeing What Isn't There   69
   How Overfitting Hurts Business   70
   Recognizing When a Model Is Overfitting   72
   The Right Balance Between Simplicity and Complexity   74
   Final Thoughts   77

5. THE DANGER OF AVERAGES ... 81
   Different Types of Averages (And Their Limitations) ... 83
   When Averages Hide Critical Insights ... 85
   Better Alternatives: Using Distributions Instead of Averages ... 87
   Rethinking the Management and Reporting Culture ... 92
   Final Thoughts ... 94

6. DASHBOARDS AND DECEPTION ... 97
   Why We're Drawn to Visual Data ... 98
   Common Techniques of Dashboard Deception ... 101
   Best Practices for Honest Dashboards ... 107
   Final Thoughts ... 110

7. MANIPULATED METRICS ... 113
   Statistics Is a Construct ... 115
   Goodhart's Law and Performance Fixation ... 116
   Vanity Metrics Versus Actionable Metrics ... 117
   Cherry picking: Creating the Narrative ... 118
   Smoothing and Moving Averages: The Fantasy of Stability ... 119
   Shifting Baselines: Moving the Goalposts ... 120
   External Spin: Manipulation Beyond the Organization ... 122
   Technical Safeguards Against Metric Manipulation ... 123
   Final Thoughts ... 125

8. COGNITIVE BIASES IN DATA ANALYSIS ... 127
   Interpretation Bias: A Human Defect ... 129
   Experience and Ingrained Patterns ... 130
   The Dangers of Dissonance ... 131
   Common Cognitive Biases in Data Analysis ... 133
   Group Dynamics: Echo Chambers and Groupthink ... 136
   Cultivating Cognitive Awareness: Defensive Strategies ... 137
   Final Thoughts ... 138

9. THE ETHICS OF DATA MANIPULATION 143
   When Does Data Manipulation Cross the Line? 144
   The Slippery Slope of Justifying Data
   Manipulation 146
   Ethical Gray Areas in Data Communication 147
   The Consequences of Unethical Data Practices 150
   Assessing the Ethics of Using Data 152
   Fundamental Principles of Ethical Data
   Management 154
   Final Thoughts 156

10. REAL-WORLD DISASTERS 159
    Financial Crises: How Bad Data Destroyed
    Economies 161
    Business Failures: When Companies Bet on the
    Wrong Data 163
    Government Failures: When Political Decisions
    Are Based on Incorrect Data 166
    Health and Science: When Bad Data Costs
    Lives 168
    Other Disasters: Beyond the Obvious 170
    Lessons Learned: Patterns and Pitfalls 172
    Final Thoughts 174

11. FIXING THE PROBLEM 175
    Step 1: Strengthen Data Pipelines to Avoid
    "Garbage In, Garbage Out" 177
    Step 2: Redesign BI Dashboards to Minimize
    Misinterpretation 179
    Step 3: Automate Data Validation and Quality
    Assurance 181
    Step 4: Prevent Overfitting and False Patterns
    in Data Models 182
    Step 5: Dealing With Complexity—Systems
    Thinking and Scenario Planning 183
    Step 6: Organizational Practices That Prevent
    Correlation Traps 185
    Step 7: Eliminate Cognitive Bias From
    Decision Making at Scale 186
    Step 8: Creating Transparent and Reliable
    Metrics 187

Embracing a Bayesian Future	188
Overcoming Implementation Challenges	189
Final Thoughts	190
12. THE FUTURE OF DECISION-MAKING	193
From Human-Driven Decisions to AI-Driven Decisions	194
The Power of Predictive Analytics	195
The Rise of AI Dashboards	197
Facing the "Black Box" Challenge	198
Protecting Against Bias and Ensuring Fairness	199
The Essential Role of Human Judgment	201
Cultivating Critical Thinking and Data Literacy	202
Decision-Making Beyond AI: Quantum Computing and Decentralization	203
Preparing For the Future: Organizational Adaptation	205
Final Thoughts	206
Conclusion	209
Glossary	213
References	217

INTRODUCTION

In the winter of 2012, as public health authorities prepared for the annual flu season, Google's much-celebrated Flu Trends tool, once hailed as the pinnacle of real-time epidemiology, issued an alarming prediction: the United States would have approximately twice as many flu cases as in a typical season.

Hospitals mobilized extra staff, pharmacies accelerated vaccine shipments, and the media amplified the warning, all based on an algorithm trained on billions of search queries. However, when the Centers for Disease Control and Prevention (CDC) released their official figures, the reality was much less dire. The incidence of flu was only marginally above average, and not the dramatic increase predicted by Google's model (Arthur, 2014).

Later, a joint team from Northeastern and Harvard revealed that Flu Trends had overestimated the prevalence of influenza in 100 of the previous 108 weeks, and, in February 2013, its prediction exceeded the actual cases reported by the

CDC by a factor of two. The researchers warned of "big data hubris": an overreliance on complex analyses whose assumptions could change in ways that wouldn't be visible until too late.

They pointed to two main sources of error: Google's own search algorithm, which made on average more than one adjustment a day, and the introduction of its "automatic suggestion" feature in November 2009. Both changes modified the volume and nature of health-related query terms, but Flu Trends was never recalibrated to take them into account.

Since Flu Trends was designed to predict CDC surveillance reports rather than measure an absolute number of flu cases, any deviation in user behavior or search indexing translated directly into misleading predictions. Even Google recognized the need for annual reviews, its last update before the 2013-14 season took place in October 2013, but the proprietary nature of the model and the lack of transparency made rigorous independent evaluation and timely recalibration virtually impossible.

What began as an impressive demonstration of the potential of data to map disease in real time has become a cautionary tale: without ongoing validation, transparency, and an understanding that correlations change over time, even the most sophisticated big data systems can mislead rather than enlighten.

In this book, we will explore how these flaws arise, not from a lack of data, but from erroneous assumptions, unexamined biases, and the seductive illusion of precision that comes with a sleek dashboard. We'll see why decision-makers must learn not only to trust their data but also to question it.

THE CENTRAL PARADOX OF DATA-DRIVEN DECISIONS

We turn to data in search of certainty, convinced that numbers can eliminate bias and reveal the objective truth. However, what happens when those same numbers are flawed, misleading, or misinterpreted?

The paradox at the heart of this book is that, in our quest to replace instinct with data-driven rigor, we often forget that the data itself is manufactured, collected, processed, and presented by fallible human hands and imperfect machines.

The modern promise of business intelligence (BI) is that precise dashboards and sophisticated algorithms can provide decision-quality answers at the click of a button. However, beneath the shiny surfaces lie hidden assumptions, corrupted data, selective reporting, and rampant cognitive biases. This book is about stripping away the veneer of apparent certainty to reveal the hidden traps that await unwary decision-makers.

But what do we mean when we talk about BI? BI is the practice of using data analysis, report generation, and dashboard visualization to guide organizational decisions. BI covers the entire spectrum, from ingesting raw data, such as retail transaction records, sensor readings from industrial equipment, click streams on a website, to generating standardized reports and implementing self-service analysis tools. It promises to transform reams of unstructured information into actionable insights, empowering executives, managers, and frontline employees to make faster, better-informed choices.

In a world of accelerating change, BI aims to be the foundation of agility, enabling companies to perceive changes in customer preferences, optimize operations, and outperform competitors.

THE EVOLUTION OF BI

In its earliest incarnations, BI meant huge piles of paper reports and manually updated spreadsheets. Data analysts spent weeks (or months) consolidating departmental figures into clunky slide shows for quarterly review meetings. Lag times of days or weeks meant that by the time insights appeared, the markets had already changed. In the last two decades, this static model has given way to centralized data warehouses and the emergence of interactive dashboards powered by OLAP (online analytical processing).

Suddenly, decision-makers could break down and analyze sales by region, product line, or time period with just a few clicks of the mouse. In the latest wave of evolution, BI has merged with artificial intelligence. Real-time analytical pipelines, predictive models trained on historical patterns, and built-in machine learning recommendations now allow companies to anticipate customer needs, detect equipment failures before they occur, and personalize marketing messages at scale.

What was once the domain of specialized analysts has become a generalized resource, with automated alerts and AI-driven insights appearing in the flow of everyday work.

WHY ORGANIZATIONS EMBRACE BI

Consider the vision: a retailer forecasting demand at the SKU level days in advance, reducing stock-outs and at the same time lowering holding costs; a hospital forecasting patient admissions to optimize staffing and avoid dangerous overcrowding; a manufacturer adjusting production schedules quickly in response to supplier delays or equipment anomalies.

BI holds the promise of transforming raw, chaotic data into signals that reduce guesswork and guide strategy. Leaders no longer need to rely solely on intuition or "best guesses"; they can base decisions on patterns derived from vast transaction histories, customer interactions, and operational telemetry. In theory, BI bridges the gap between data overload and clear action, allowing organizations to continuously adapt to changing markets and emerging risks.

"Data-driven decision making" has become the mantra of modern companies, from Silicon Valley startups to global financial institutions. BI is seen as a competitive advantage: in hyper-competitive sectors, the ability to identify trends a day earlier or a margin or two tighter can translate into millions of dollars.

In addition to the promise of profitability, the numbers give a veneer of objectivity and impartiality. When executives cite precise metrics: "We achieved a 3.62% reduction in turnover," the language of decimals stifles disagreement and reduces debate.

Along with the rise of automation and AI, organizations now believe they can process oceans of data in real time, revealing insights that were previously hidden or invisible. If a dashboard can flag up a problem that's brewing before any human being notices, why wouldn't every leader demand it?

The dirty secret of BI is that analysis does not guarantee accuracy, and interpretation does not guarantee insight. A dashboard can be very well designed, but fundamentally misleading. Algorithms can discover spurious correlations that fall apart under scrutiny. Models can overfit previous data and completely fail under new conditions.

Cognitive biases such as anchoring, confirmation, and availability bias permeate the analytical process, from data collection to final presentation. Organizations enthusiastically adopt BI tools, only to repeat the same strategic mistakes more quickly and on a larger scale. The question is not whether to use data, but how to recognize when data is leading us astray.

WHAT THIS BOOK IS (AND ISN'T)

How can decision-makers recognize and avoid the hidden pitfalls of BI before making costly mistakes? What practical steps can organizations take to ensure that their dashboards reflect, rather than distort, reality? How do cognitive biases distort our interpretation of graphs and reports, and how can we protect ourselves against these mental traps? What ethical barriers should be built around data collection, modeling, and reporting to avoid the manipulation (intentional or not) of critical metrics? This book explores these questions, showing the anatomy of BI failures and the psychology behind misplaced trust in numbers.

This is not an instruction guide for specific BI software, such as Tableau or Power BI. Nor is it a general textbook on data science algorithms or coding techniques. Instead, it's an exploration of why BI can fool even the most well-intentioned organizations and how to protect yourself against these dangers.

Through real-world case studies, from algorithmic trading losses to public health blunders such as Google Flu Trends, psychological insights into human biases, and practical frameworks for rigorous data governance, this book offers a roadmap for avoiding BI disasters. Here you won't find step-by-step tutorials; you'll become aware of the hidden forces that can derail data-driven strategies and learn practical methods for creating more reliable analyses.

This book is essential reading for business leaders and executives who rely on BI reports to make high-risk decisions and need to understand the limits of data. Analysts and data professionals will find guidance on how to present numbers ethically and transparently, as well as how to avoid common modeling pitfalls. Students and researchers can deepen their understanding of the pitfalls of BI beyond the technical aspects of statistics, learning why real-world data problems often defy textbook solutions.

Finally, anyone who has uncritical faith in dashboards and numerical summaries will benefit from a more skeptical and questioning approach, developing the critical skills needed to separate meaningful insights from statistical mirages.

A FINAL NOTE BEFORE THE START

In an age flooded with data and seduced by promises of precision, the best decision-makers will not be those who trust every graph or algorithm available. They will be those who know when to question the numbers, who recognize that data, at all stages, is constructed, filtered, and often flawed.

The central message of this book is simple but profound: the most powerful skill in a data-driven world is knowing when to doubt the data. Only by combining rigorous analytical methods with human judgment, ethical vigilance, and a culture of constructive skepticism can organizations fulfill the true promise of BI: turning data into decisions that are not only faster and more cost-effective but also wiser and more resilient.

CHAPTER 1

THE ILLUSION OF ACCURACY

> *The weaker the data available upon which to base one's conclusion, the greater the precision which should be quoted in order to give the data authenticity.*
>
> — NORMAN RALPH AUGUSTINE

Numbers have a way of captivating us like nothing else in business and everyday life. When a salesperson announces a projection of 16.3% growth in quarterly revenue, we feel it's truer than if he simply said, "We think sales will increase by around 15 or 20%."

We see decimal points and assume that a rigorous process has been carried out: data has been collected, models have been run, and each step has been a meticulous progression that has led us to an indisputable truth. Precision, or at least its appearance, instantly creates a sense of authority. And because we generally respect authority, exact numbers can short-circuit our natural inclination to question and doubt.

And why is that? Much of it stems from the way we've been taught to see math and science. From an early age, we learn that numbers represent solid, factual knowledge. The multiplication table never lies, and a geometry problem solved correctly will always represent an accurate answer.

This sense of certainty becomes ingrained in our thought processes. In a world full of ambiguities, especially in business, politics, and social problems, numbers are like islands of stability. So a pie chart detailing a 27.45% customer conversion rate will comfort us: "Finally something real," we tell ourselves, "something measured, beyond debate."

This cultural training, which treats numbers as facts, sets the stage for what becomes a deep-rooted trust, almost like a *spell* of accuracy. We assume that a specific decimal or percentage will be the last word and that everything behind it has been done correctly. Over time, this can foster a dangerous environment where decisions depend on a superficial appearance of statistical rigor and "evidence-based" rather than a genuine understanding of how the numbers were produced.

It doesn't help that, in many professional environments, questioning a meticulously formatted spreadsheet or a well-presented dashboard is socially awkward or, worse, career-limiting. It's normal to be afraid of questioning and, in the end, to appear unprepared and even anti-scientific. The norm is to nod in agreement, especially if the figures appear in official documents or come from someone considered an expert. As a result, even glaring inconsistencies or assumptions that skip too many steps can remain hidden in plain sight, overshadowed by the hypnotic power of decimals.

On top of all this, our appetite for accurate-sounding data has intensified as organizations have become more "data-driven." During strategy meetings and project presentations, being able to say, "We forecast a 3.62% reduction in operating costs," can be far more persuasive than the best anecdotal evidence. Team members eagerly adopt analytical tools to stand out, producing metrics that look impressive but may be based on weak premises. The more elaborate the methodology, the harder it is to discover the flaws hidden in layers of code, logical statements, and statistical assumptions.

Despite all this, precision is not an enemy per se, of course. We're not here to fight against science and numbers, but against the *uncritical acceptance* that leads to failure. In the following sections, we'll dig deeper into why those decimal numbers can fool us so easily, how hidden assumptions lurk behind many numbers, and how a lack of context can turn a true statistic into a half-truth. We'll also see how an unquestioning faith in "facts and figures" can backfire, damaging both our individual decision-making and entire organizational cultures.

THE PSYCHOLOGICAL COMFORT OF PRECISION

When a person claims to have accurate information, we instinctively trust them more. This is because our brains value specificity as evidence of expertise. Consider, for example, a doctor who tells you that your treatment has a 77% chance of success, while another tells you that the chances are "between 70 and 80%." Although the second doctor is reflecting the uncertainty more honestly, we tend to trust the first doctor's precise statement more.

This phenomenon has its roots in cognitive psychology. *We prefer confidence to ambiguity*, and exact numbers give the impression of confidence (Jerez-Fernandez et al., 2013). However, this preference ignores the real possibility that the difference between 70% and 77% may be based on nothing more than a statistical difference by different models or a different data set, perhaps one that is out of date or has poor sampling. This blinding effect of specificity can lead to a sense of complacency, where we are willing to assume that if something has been measured and reported, then it must be accurate.

In business, entire presentations can hinge on how accurately you've presented a forecast. One product manager might say, "Market research shows an annual growth of 31.5% for this segment," while another manager addresses the same trend by mentioning "approximately 30% growth." Although both may be referring to the same data, the manager with the decimal-laden statement usually sounds more credible. Executives, pressed for time and eager for concrete guidance, may cling to the first number as if it were an unquestionable fact.

Studies also show that more confident people make more precise estimates than less confident people (Jerez-Fernandez et al., 2013). And just as precise figures seem more reliable, we trust people who seem more confident. This is very clear when we see political choices, where people tend to believe in those who speak more confidently, even if what they say isn't true.

Another force that fuels the allure of exact numbers is the perceived complexity of the analysis behind them (Xie & Kronrod, 2012). If a data science team has run a sophisticated model, incorporating machine learning, advanced regressions, or multiple data streams, then the results should be robust, right?

Unfortunately, complexity can be a smokescreen. The more elaborate the methodology, the easier it is to hide errors or questionable assumptions. Think of it like a magic trick: complexity distracts the audience, making them less likely to notice the hidden moves. As a result, executives and stakeholders see 31.5% and assume it must be the product of an airtight calculation, forgetting that sophisticated models can be wrong in sophisticated ways.

Of course, there are situations where specificity is beneficial, especially in well-established scientific or engineering contexts where margins of error can be carefully quantified. For example, if an aircraft engineer claims that a critical component can withstand exactly 2,500 pounds of force, that figure is probably backed up by rigorous testing and standardized protocols. When making commercial or strategic decisions, however, data sources are generally much more fluid. Markets change, consumer tastes evolve, and even the definitions of success or failure can change from one quarter to the next.

To complicate matters, some people learn to use precision as a weapon. A manager can increase confidence in a shaky forecast by presenting it with decimal points to create authority. Sports experts discuss National Football League draft prospects in hundredths of milliseconds (more precision than measurement error allows). By sprinkling decimals and complex terminology into a report, they take advantage of the well-known tendency that precision means reliability.

Ultimately, the danger lies in confusing detailed figures with accurate perceptions. We need to remember that all measurements, however precise they may seem, come with a margin of error, an uncertainty that can only be verified if you read the methodological notes or footnotes that few people bother to look at. Our willingness to accept numbers when they look impressive can lead us to ignore important responsibilities about how they were obtained or what real-world contingencies might invalidate them.

THE ROLE OF ASSUMPTIONS IN DATA ACCURACY

Numbers never just appear out of thin air. There is always a data collection methodology or procedure, with human assumptions and judgments. These assumptions and judgments are often hidden in spreadsheets, codes, and in the minds of those carrying out the analysis. The result is a simple, easily digestible number or percentage that appears on slides, conversations, and memos. But as soon as we accept that number without examining its basis, we open ourselves up to potential disasters.

Take this example: An analyst is forecasting holiday sales. He may assume that the company's target audience will continue to spend at the same rate as the previous year, ignoring emerging trends such as a new competitor or a change in consumer sentiment. The final forecast may seem very clear in a report, "Projected 18% increase in holiday revenue," but it is based on an increasingly unstable premise.

If the next assumption doesn't hold up, the 18% figure will be little more than a guess.

The problem is compounded when several assumptions pile on top of each other. In data science, it's not uncommon to have dozens of input variables and constraints feeding into a single model. Even if each assumption seems small, such as expecting labor costs to remain constant or assuming that your supply chain will run smoothly, the cumulative effect can be enormous.

A single incorrect assumption can render an entire analysis unreliable. When analysts or decision-makers don't highlight these assumptions, the final figures look much more certain than they really are.

A recent study of German GDP forecasts found that around 75% of the variation in forecast errors was due to inaccuracies in initial assumptions (Heinisch et al., 2024). This suggests that erroneous assumptions, not just miscalculations, are the root cause of many misleading projections. The researchers emphasized that greater transparency in the disclosure of assumptions would make forecasts more useful, especially when shaping political or strategic decisions.

What's more, assumptions sometimes reveal a subtle bias in the way data is interpreted. For example, a company that has historically been successful in a particular strategy may assume that it can replicate that success in a new market. The figures may then reflect this internal optimism, presenting a supposedly "data-driven" case for expansion.

However, if the new market has totally different cultural norms or regulatory environments, this assumption may not work. The resulting illusion of precision becomes an automatically reinforcing prophecy: the more numbers that seem to confirm the expansion plan, the less anyone questions the basic premise.

In an ideal world, each number would be accompanied by a transparent list of caveats: "This forecast assumes stable oil prices," "Our analysis only uses data from urban regions," or "We have adjusted for past anomalies in consumer behavior, but new disruptions may occur."

Of course, these disclaimers rarely make it into the final set of slides. Even when they do, they can be relegated to small footnotes or overshadowed by pretty graphics. Thus, many organizations move forward on the strength of numbers that appear to be set in stone but in reality rest on a fragile network of "ifs" and "maybes".

Why don't we challenge these assumptions more often? One reason is that it's time-consuming and uncomfortable. Asking a presenter to detail all their assumptions can feel confrontational, especially in a business culture that values efficiency and decisiveness.

Another reason is that exposing assumptions often reveals how provisional many figures really are. This can undermine trust and create a sense of unease. Ironically, however, a culture that openly discusses assumptions is generally more resilient and less prone to catastrophic decisions. It fosters an environment in which figures serve as starting points for discussion rather than final verdicts on what to do next.

WHY CONTEXT IS EVERYTHING

Even the most accurate statistic can be misleading if it is not anchored in context. Consider a headline that announces "50% more web traffic this month!" Sounds like a big win until you find out that last month's traffic was low due to a website problem. Without this contextual detail, the figure shows a distorted picture of success. The same goes for financial metrics, operational data, or even basic key performance indicators (KPIs) in an organization.

Context involves understanding the conditions under which the data was collected, the baseline for comparison, and the historical or external factors that can influence the result. Separating a number from its wider story is like taking a single sentence from a book and then judging the whole book solely based on that fragment. The sentence may be accurate, but it doesn't convey the full meaning of what's going on.

In business presentations, figures are usually displayed in isolation for the sake of simplicity and brevity. A graph may show a steady upward trend in the number of monthly users of a product, suggesting good growth. But if the population of potential users has also increased dramatically, for example, because the company has expanded into a new region, then some of this growth may just be a side effect of having a larger market and not necessarily a reflection of the product's appeal. Without clarifying this dynamic, the graph can be misleading. Executives may conclude that the product is performing better than it actually is.

Time periods can also distort the interpretation. For example, if a sales team shows a large quarterly increase in closed deals, this may seem impressive until you realize that they are comparing the best quarter of the year with a historically weak quarter or that they have advanced deals to meet a deadline. Similarly, if a statistic says that "30% of customers surveyed prefer our brand," you need to know how, when, and where these customers were surveyed. If the survey was only carried out among frequent buyers, the 30% figure may not reflect the general market.

A particularly misleading type of context omission occurs when people select data to highlight success. They may show a favorable metric and conveniently leave out the bigger picture. For example, a company claims that "revenue grew by 20% in the last fiscal year," but avoids mentioning that its profit margins plummeted during the same period, turning that revenue growth into a net loss. In this sense, the 20% figure may be correct, strictly speaking, but the incomplete context makes it dangerously misleading.

The solution is not to abandon the use of numbers or start flooding every report with a hundred disclaimers. Instead, it's about cultivating a mindset of curiosity. When a single impressive number appears, the immediate question should be: *"Under what conditions is this number true?"* This simple question can lead to a follow-up on the baseline, the comparison groups, the exceptions, the historical trends, or even the units of measurement. Sometimes, the context reveals that the number is genuinely good news; other times, it shows that the apparent good news is more complex or less certain than the headline suggests.

What's more, providing context can actually increase confidence in a team's analysis. By openly addressing the factors that could shape or alter the meaning of the data, analysts demonstrate rigor. They indicate that they have analyzed various angles and are not trying to hide inconvenient details. This level of transparency often results in greater buy-in from stakeholders, who appreciate the recognition that reality rarely fits neatly into a single metric.

THE EFFECTS OF BLIND TRUST

So far, we've seen that numbers can enchant us through their perceived accuracy, obscure layers of assumptions, and lack of context. But what happens when organizations systematically rely too much on these numbers? The repercussions can extend far beyond a single misstep; they can shape a company's culture and strategy in profound ways.

One of the biggest risks is the *misallocation of resources.* If executives read a great report that quotes an accurate 12.6% expected return on a new product line, they may allocate budget and staff based on the strength of that figure. However, if that 12.6% is based on questionable assumptions (such as stable prices or unwavering customer loyalty), the reality could be totally different. The company may discover, only too late, that it has invested time and money in something that never had a solid foundation. Meanwhile, really promising initiatives may go unfunded because they weren't accompanied by equally convincing, but possibly inflated, figures.

Another concern is *overconfidence.* When teams see data that seems to confirm their strategy, they may stop investigating alternative points of view or possible pitfalls. Simply having a number can create a sense of finality, as if the analysis has been "proven." In rapidly changing markets, an organization that clings too rigidly to a supposedly accurate forecast can be surprised by emerging trends. It doesn't adapt in time because the data told it was on the right track, despite real-world signs suggesting otherwise.

Blind trust also erodes teams' critical thinking skills. If the norm is to accept any number that appears on a well-made PowerPoint, people may stop questioning or learning. Over time, this fosters a culture where people expect the answers to be provided by the data, forgetting that *judgment* and *experience* still play integral roles in interpreting these data points. Employees may be afraid to challenge the data, worried that they will appear pessimistic or problematic, especially in cultures that idolize "data-driven."

In addition, an unshakeable belief in numbers can *damage relationships with external stakeholders* (investors, customers, and the public) if those numbers don't pan out. Overly optimistic forecasts, quoted to the decimal point, can raise expectations unrealistically. When reality diverges, as it often does, the company looks incompetent or deceitful. Trust, once lost, can be difficult to rebuild. In extreme cases, regulatory bodies can intervene if they suspect that financial forecasts or public statements have been misleading.

There is also a subtle but significant *emotional cost for employees*. Suppose a sales team is told that it must achieve a target formulated on the basis of an ultra-precise growth rate. If the team realizes that these figures are unattainable or based on wrong assumptions, their morale can plummet.

They see the target as an impossible standard. However, management may insist, convinced by the "hard data." This disconnect generates frustration, burnout, and a feeling of disillusionment in the workforce.

Finally, the more an organization is hypnotized by numerical accuracy, the more it risks *missing out on quality insights*. Customer interviews and observational data often contain good clues about changing preferences or emerging trends. This information can be confusing and difficult to quantify, but it often offers early warnings or highlights opportunities that a purely numbers-based approach might overlook. By ignoring or devaluing this information, leaders lock themselves into a narrow view that may be quite accurate, but is far from comprehensive.

FINAL THOUGHTS

Numbers can shape decisions, reveal patterns, and guide strategic discussions. There's a reason data analysis has become essential in modern business: it often allows us to identify inefficiencies, track performance, and predict scenarios in a way that instinct simply cannot. However, with this power comes the responsibility to remain vigilant. Precision can quickly become an illusion if we neglect its assumptions, take it out of context, or forget that numbers are just *one* piece of the wider decision-making puzzle.

To deal with this effectively, we need a balanced approach. Firstly, we can cultivate a *mindset of healthy skepticism*. Whenever a statistic seems too good (or bad) to be true or is presented with an air of absolute certainty, we should be willing to look under the hood: Where did the data come from? How was it processed? What real-world conditions could invalidate these results?

Organizations that excel in the effective use of data generally encourage this kind of questioning as an integral part of their culture. They encourage analysts to articulate all the assumptions they have made, specify the data sources, note the margin of error, and highlight possible limitations. Leaders in such environments don't see these discussions as an obstacle; they see them as *essential due diligence* that avoids costly mistakes.

Another practice is to *avoid presenting a single number in isolation*. Instead, show ranges, confidence intervals, or various scenarios. This approach shows that the future is uncertain and that data can only provide probabilities, not certainties. While it's tempting to present a single number for maximum impact, this can rob stakeholders of the chance to understand all possible outcomes.

We must also remember that numbers serve human beings, not the other way around. Human judgment, creativity, and adaptability are still irreplaceable. When we rely too much on numerical precision, we run the risk of ignoring signals that cannot be reduced to decimal numbers, such as changes in consumer sentiment, cultural nuances, or ethical considerations. Balancing quantitative insights with qualitative perspectives allows for a more holistic view, reducing the risk of illusions that could otherwise get out of hand.

In short, the illusion of precision doesn't arise because numbers are inherently misleading, but because we often give them a certainty, they don't deserve. A conscious approach that respects the potential of data but never treats it as infallible is the surest way to capture the true benefits of quantitative insights.

However, there is a deeper layer: sometimes our data is broken from the start, riddled with omissions, errors, or biases so severe that no amount of statistical subtlety can save it. That's what we turn to in the next chapter, exploring how *"bad data"* infiltrates our systems, how it distorts the numbers we trust, and why even the best analysis can't overcome such a flawed foundation.

CHAPTER 2

GARBAGE IN, GARBAGE OUT

> *Garbage in, garbage out. Or rather more felicitously: the tree of nonsense is watered with error, and from its branches swing the pumpkins of disaster.*
>
> — NICK HARKAWAY

We've said that data isn't inherently misleading, but it can be "bad" from the start, and that can be counterintuitive. After all, we usually imagine data as neutral, a reflection of reality that just needs to be measured and recorded. However, the phrase "garbage in, garbage out" (GIGO) encapsulates a simple truth: *No matter how advanced your analysis, flawed inputs will produce flawed outputs.*

In other words, if the fundamental data is incomplete, inaccurate, biased, or irrelevant, any insight or decision derived from it will inevitably be compromised. It's not about illusions of precision or decimal points that look impressive. Instead, it's about the basic building blocks of the evidence itself, what it represents, how it is collected, and whether it can be trusted.

Think of data as the ingredients in a kitchen. Even a world-class chef, armed with incredible equipment and creative recipes, will struggle to prepare a truly exceptional meal if the ingredients are spoiled. You can decorate the dish, garnish it with fine herbs, and serve it on luxurious crockery, but behind it all lies a fundamental flaw: the food never had a chance to be delicious because it started out spoiled.

The same principle applies to analytics. You can invest in sophisticated algorithms or "big data" platforms, but if the information is contaminated, the results simply won't be reliable.

In practice, "garbage data" takes many forms: missing or incomplete entries, errors introduced by human negligence, entire categories of distorted records, misaligned definitions between teams, or data that is technically correct but totally irrelevant to the questions at hand.

And while it may seem that small errors can be ignored or corrected later, the reality is much more dangerous. Data pipelines can be incredibly complex. A small error introduced early in the process can grow, deform, or contaminate multiple data sets as it spreads throughout an organization. Once a dashboard is on the ground, no one remembers that the numbers in it were built on half-truths and assumptions, which ultimately leads to misguided strategies or empty successes.

This chapter explores the various nuances of this type of data, showing what makes it so dangerous and why even well-intentioned attempts to clean it up may not solve the fundamental problems. We'll examine the common points where bad data creeps in, whether through manual processes or automated systems, and show how an overemphasis on quantity over quality can amplify rather than mitigate data problems.

DATA AS A REFLECTION OF REALITY (OR NOT)

In an ideal world, every piece of data we collect would be a mirror image of reality. If you were tracking a store's sales, each transaction record would accurately report the amount, date, product ID, and payment type. If you were analyzing customer behavior, every demographic or preference field would be filled in with the correct information. Unfortunately, reality is not so organized. People make mistakes, machines malfunction, definitions conflict, and contexts change. Over time, the data set you thought mirrored reality begins to diverge from the truth in subtle ways, sometimes so subtly, that you don't notice the gap until it becomes too big to ignore.

One of the most overlooked factors is *time lag*. Data that was accurate last quarter can become obsolete. Market dynamics change, new product lines emerge, consumer preferences evolve, and the data you were so confident of no longer represents the current situation. The "lag" can be just weeks or months, but even a short period can be enough to turn relevant insights into outdated relics. And if no one in the organization signals the change, because all departments are busy or assume that someone else is in charge of updating the information, this once accurate data moves into "garbage" territory.

What's more, the data is usually collected under *varying protocols*. One department might define an "active user" as anyone who has logged into an application in the last 30 days. Another department might define it as anyone who has simply opened an email newsletter. When these two departments merge or share analytics, the incompatibility in definitions can create a single combined data set full of duplications, contradictions, and meaningless averages. From a distance, everything still looks numerical and objective, but it doesn't correspond to a single coherent reality.

The important thing here is that data rarely exists in a vacuum. They are generated by processes, some manual, others automated, which involve human decisions at various stages. What is measured, how it is measured, and who is responsible for capturing or verifying it all affect the final data set. This means that there are a wide variety of opportunities for "garbage" to be entered, either deliberately (as in the case of manipulated numbers) or accidentally (as in the case of well-intentioned but inconsistent data entry). Understanding these complexities is the first step in recognizing why the label "garbage in, garbage out" is so widespread.

WHAT MAKES DATA "GARBAGE" IN THE FIRST PLACE?

"Garbage data" is an umbrella term. It can refer to subtle, almost invisible errors that slightly skew the accuracy of a data set or to massive gaps that invalidate entire fields of analysis. Let's break down the various forms that poor-quality data can take, each of which has its own challenges.

Incomplete Data

Incomplete data can be the most common form of garbage. Consider a simple scenario: a customer signs up for a product review but doesn't fill in their email address. This is a missing field in a sea of potential entries; harmless, right?

But what if 30% of sign-ups do the same, and your team is trying to measure lead conversion through email engagement? Suddenly, a large part of the data you rely on to measure performance can't be used. You can try to "fix" this by extrapolating from the data you have or ignoring the missing entries altogether, but you run the risk of distorting the results.

Incomplete data also appears when certain variables are optional or when systems experience a period of inactivity that prevents recording. A marketing analytics platform may not be able to track web traffic accurately if a piece of code on the site is broken. Thousands of visits may not be recorded, and the team analyzing the data may see a false drop in traffic. They respond by revamping a campaign that was actually working well, all because they believed the incomplete data told a true story.

Inaccurate Data

While incomplete data means missing fields, inaccurate data means that the fields exist but don't tell the truth. This can happen for a number of reasons: a typo inserts an extra zero into a sales number, an outdated address remains in the file, or a sensor failure causes readings to consistently fall outside a certain margin. The difference with incomplete data is that nobody notices that anything is missing; it's there, it's just wrong.

A single inaccurate record may not have a major cascading effect unless, of course, it is a critical record used for budgeting or forecasting. However, inaccurate data often appears in groups.

Imagine a situation where a transportation company makes the transition to a new tracking system. In the process, the data conversion scripts incorrectly map the old tracking codes to the new system, so thousands of shipments end up with scrambled destination records.

Over time, this jumble of shipment data is used to assess performance on various routes. Entire logistics plans may be based on random or inconsistent codes, and the organization may decide to reduce capacity in areas where the system claims demand is low, although in fact it is the data that is scrambled.

Biased or Distorted Data

Biased data is more subtle. Rather than being obviously incomplete or incorrect, the data set may appear legitimate on the surface. However, the sample from which it was collected *does not represent* the actual population or phenomenon that one wishes to understand.

For example, a workplace morale survey distributed only via an optional email link may attract responses mainly from employees who love or hate their job, leaving out the moderate majority. Or consider an e-commerce site that only tracks feedback from shoppers who proactively rate their purchases, ignoring the silent majority who don't have a strong opinion or don't find the rating system easy to use.

Biased data is particularly pernicious because it often *masquerades as authentic*. Perhaps you have 10,000 responses, all carefully recorded and verified. The data set is huge and may seem robust. However, if those 10,000 responses come from a skewed subset of your customer base, your analysis could completely ignore what the majority of your customers want or feel. Worse still, the more confident you feel about "big data", the easier it is to ignore the possibility of bias.

Irrelevant or Noisy Data

Finally, there is data that, while not necessarily incorrect or missing, is not really important to the problem at hand. With the rise of big data platforms, many organizations fall into the trap of accumulating all the information they can: social media posts, website logs, customer interactions, sensor readings, with the assumption that "we might need it one day". In reality, collecting everything can bury your analysts in huge, heavy data sets.

Imagine trying to find the right screws in a drawer full of nails, screws, washers, and random junk. Time spent sorting out irrelevant bits is time not spent searching for the data points that really matter. Noisy data can lead to false correlations and patterns and *analysis paralysis*, where the sheer volume of information overwhelms the ability to gain meaningful insights (Forester, 2023). Data that doesn't serve a clear purpose is effectively garbage, even if it has been meticulously collected and stored.

HOW BAD DATA GETS COLLECTED?

If garbage data is so dangerous, it's worth asking: *where does it really come from?* The sources are numerous and often mundane. In many organizations, data collection processes grow organically. Initially, a small team might keep a few spreadsheets with basic columns. Over time, as the company expands, these spreadsheets are linked to external databases, or employees start recording information on new software platforms. Each transition is an opportunity for errors or incompatibilities, typos, misaligned fields, or sloppy merges.

Human error is perhaps the most obvious culprit. Anyone who has ever manually entered a long stream of numbers into a spreadsheet knows how easy it is to get distracted and enter a digit incorrectly. In addition to typos, employees can misinterpret instructions about which fields should be filled in or overlook certain data points due to a lack of time. Small errors accumulate, especially when there are no robust validation steps to detect them. Overworked or undertrained team members become part-time data entry clerks, and the system is expected to "self-correct" at some point in the process.

But it's not just about manual entry. *Automated systems* can also produce incorrect data when they are not properly calibrated or maintained. In the retail sector, for example, a point-of-sale system may record each sale with a timestamp, item code, and total value. If a software update introduces a bug that incorrectly interprets certain item codes, thousands of transactions could be mislabeled. By the time the error appears in a monthly report, the data has already been processed with faulty information, making it harder to separate the good records from the bad.

A third factor, often overlooked, is *organizational silos*. Different departments may use different software tools or naming conventions, turning data consolidation into a chaotic "tower of Babel". One team calls a product category "Smartwatches", while another calls it "Wearables", and a third groups it under "Electronics". When these data sets converge, the system can treat them as separate items or forcibly merge them into a single category, hiding the nuances. Over time, confusing classification leads to miscounted inventories, inaccurate sales metrics, and bad forecasts.

Data pipeline dispersion is another phenomenon that can introduce useless data. As an organization grows, it can add more and more data transformations: one script to clean and normalize text fields, another script to integrate external data sources, a third to run preliminary analyses, and so on. Each script has the potential to alter, delete, or misinterpret certain values. Unless someone diligently monitors each step, you end up with a "pipeline of errors", where mistakes from previous steps are magnified in later ones.

Finally, *a lack of accountability* often cements the problem of useless data. If no individual or team is clearly responsible for ensuring data integrity at every stage, everyone assumes that someone else is in charge. Problems fester, go unreported, or go unnoticed. The moment a glaring inconsistency arises, perhaps a KPI that logically can't be correct, people scramble to find out where in the pipeline the error originated. This after-the-fact detective work can be painstaking, and the damage (such as a wrong decision or erroneous public statement) is often already done.

THE HIDDEN DANGER OF "FIXING" DATA

"Just clean the data". This is a common argument in organizations that discover faults. The idea is simple: ask analysts or data engineers to scour the dataset, fill in the blanks, correct obvious errors, remove duplicates, and perhaps run some algorithmic method to smooth or interpolate missing points. After that, the data is supposedly "ready" for analysis. Unfortunately, the cleaning process often introduces new risks or simply masks deeper problems.

Cosmetic Fixes vs Root Problems

One of the main pitfalls is that "cleaning" can be purely cosmetic. Suppose a column in your sales database is missing 20% of its entries. An eager analyst might decide to fill in these missing fields by averaging the known entries. Mathematically, this sounds simple; there are no more blank cells, and the final data set can be run through the analysis pipeline without generating errors.

But in reality, those 20% of missing values may have had totally different characteristics from the known subset. By assuming that they correspond to the average, you have effectively invented data that may not reflect any real event or transaction. *The root cause:* why these records were missing in the first place, remains unresolved.

Reinforcing Biases

Cleaning procedures can also *reinforce existing biases*. If your training dataset already under-represents a certain demographic group, any interpolation method can further dilute its presence in the dataset, making it even less visible in the final result. Similarly, outlier removal techniques, designed to eliminate spurious data points, can ironically remove legitimate but less common observations. This can hide the fact that your product has a niche but significant group of users, or that certain geographical regions behave differently from the norm. By labeling these as "outliers" and eliminating them, you rid your data set of potentially enlightening variation.

The Transparency Gap

Another concern is the *lack of transparency* about what exactly was done during the cleaning. Imagine a manager or executive looking at a final report that says: "We have a complete dataset of 20,000 customer records". In reality, perhaps only 15,000 are really complete, and 5,000 have been "cleaned" by filling in missing fields with assumptions.

If the final report does not reveal this proportion, senior leadership may operate under the illusion that all 20,000 records are equally reliable. Critical decisions can then be made based on a false premise that each line item is a real, verified record, and not an estimate. Over time, these undisclosed manipulations create a climate in which people blindly trust the data system, unaware of how tenuous some of its numbers may be.

Data Pipeline Inertia

Once data has been "cleaned", it usually moves on to the next stages: aggregations, visualizations, or advanced analysis. Each subsequent stage assumes that the input is reliable. When data goes through several transformations, it is extremely difficult to retrace the steps back to the original raw inputs. If a question arises, "Why does our monthly revenue data show these anomalies?", teams may have to dig through multiple scripts or documentation (if it exists at all) to find out which cleaning procedure introduced the discrepancy. Meanwhile, the company may be moving forward with decisions based on a set of processed data that no one fully understands.

WHY MORE DATA DOESN'T MEAN BETTER DATA

A natural response to the GIGO principle is: "Of course, some of our data may be flawed, but we have so much data in general that it should balance out." This is a tempting mindset because, in many fields of research, larger samples reduce variation and produce more accurate estimates. However, this is only true when the data is *consistently collected, representative, and accurate*. If the underlying data streams are riddled with systematic errors, biases, or irrelevancies, accumulating more data simply amplifies the garbage.

Scaling Up Errors

When an organization invests in "big data" solutions, it usually aggregates data from various sources: social media feeds, transactional records, third-party APIs, sensor readings, etc. Each source can contribute its own form of garbage, spam accounts, poorly programmed sensors, partial records of network outages, and so on.

Far from canceling each other out, these errors can compound each other. The integrated data set may seem comprehensive, but it is full of inaccurate or redundant points. Analysts spend weeks or months sifting through the noise, only to end up with questionable correlations or spurious patterns.

Analysis Paralysis

Another disadvantage of fixating on quantity is the risk of what we mentioned earlier, analysis paralysis. Teams end up drowning in data, hoping that advanced analytics or machine learning algorithms will identify "the truth" hidden in it. However, when the proportion of garbage is high, or the data is hopelessly inconsistent, advanced algorithms simply end up chasing random fluctuations.

Without a robust sense of quality control, the complexity of big data can generate a maze of meaningless patterns. This not only wastes time, but can also create a false confidence among decision-makers who see sophisticated models in action without realizing how much garbage those models have had to ingest.

False Sense of Security

Big Data initiatives usually come with a significant investment in infrastructure. Data lakes, distributed storage systems, streaming pipelines; they can cost millions to install and maintain. Once this money has been spent, there is psychological and organizational pressure to justify the investment by producing results.

This environment can foster a dangerous complacency: "We have the biggest data available, so our conclusions must be valid." The presence of advanced tools and large volumes of data can act as a smokescreen, preventing the important questions: "Are we sure we trust each source? Are we sure the data is relevant and accurate?"

WHY GIGO STILL PERSISTS?

One of the main reasons why GIGO continues has less to do with the data itself and more to do with the *cultures and behaviors* that surround it. Many organizations favor speed over verification, sending the message that data quality is not the top priority.

Under constant pressure to produce flashy metrics or urgent reports, teams may grab all the numbers they can and present them as conclusive, ignoring deeper checks such as validation or cross-referencing. Over time, this "just do it" mentality normalizes partially verified or totally unverified data, causing entire processes to be built on hidden inaccuracies.

In addition to this challenge, *data ownership is often ambiguous.* It may oversee the infrastructure, business units may handle the daily input, and analysts may run the actual reports, but no one is clearly responsible for quality control. When a glaring discrepancy arises, it's not clear which group is to blame or who has the power to correct it. Meanwhile, some companies rely on a single "data guru" to maintain everything. If this person leaves or has their own prejudices, a dangerous monopoly on knowledge can accelerate the spread of faulty data.

Even when people spot inconsistencies, resolving them can be a painstaking and unglamorous task. Ensuring data integrity doesn't produce dramatic headlines or instant revenue, so it rarely gets the organization's spotlight. Some leaders also fear that a full audit may reveal more problems than they are prepared to deal with, especially if they have built high-risk decisions on supposedly solid metrics. As a result, they move on and hope that incremental adjustments will fix any gaps, an approach that rarely addresses the root causes.

Finally, as companies become more "data-driven" and integrate external sources or AI systems, the consequences of GIGO can grow exponentially. Information from social media platforms or government databases may be outdated, incomplete, or based on narrow definitions. Machine learning algorithms, in turn, can amplify these hidden distortions in thousands or millions of automated decisions, from product recommendations to credit approvals. No model can overcome the quality of its input data, making faulty data a challenge for the entire industry and not just an internal organizational problem.

Recognizing GIGO Red Flags

While it may seem disheartening that there are so many ways for useless data to thrive, organizations can at least learn to identify certain "red flags" that indicate a possible GIGO problem.

We're not prescribing detailed solutions (those will be found in Chapter 11) but simply pointing out the early warning signs that data may not be what it seems:

- **Missing fields or frequent default values:** If 40% of your entries in a critical data set have standard placeholders (such as "N/A" or "Unknown"), this is a telltale sign that you may be basing decisions on incomplete information.
- **Unexplained rises or falls:** A sudden rise or fall in an important metric with no parallel real-world event (such as a marketing campaign or economic change) suggests a recording error, a system bug, or a data merge gone wrong.
- **Inconsistent definitions between reports:** If one report states that you have 10,000 "active users" and another states that you have 15,000, but both refer to the same time period, this implies a mismatch of criteria or labels. This incompatibility is GIGO's main territory.
- **Excessive use of "clean" or "interpolated" labels:** Although some cleaning is inevitable, be careful if large parts of your dataset are described as "imputed" or "automatically corrected". The larger this part, the more constructed your final numbers may be.

- **No documented pipeline:** If you ask how the data goes from the raw collection to the final report, and no one can give you a detailed overview, you're probably dealing with an opaque pipeline. Opacity is a breeding ground for errors and hidden assumptions.

Recognizing these warning signs is half the battle. Once you've seen them, you can start asking questions and digging deeper to uncover the root causes rather than blindly trusting the final figures.

FINAL THOUGHTS

Chapter 1 showed how we can be enchanted by exact-looking numbers and trust blindly with the precision of decimal points. This chapter then revealed a deeper threat: the data itself can be unreliable, riddled with omissions, mislabeling, or outright errors. Together, these pitfalls expose a common danger: making critical decisions based on illusions, whether they stem from faulty assumptions or simply incorrect data.

Just as faith in perfect-sounding projections can lead an organization to overinvest in the wrong strategy, garbage data can silently distort entire pipelines, eroding trust and fueling costly mistakes. When you consider the wide variety of garbage data, such as missing fields, incorrect entries, biased samples, and irrelevant noise, it's clear that no single fix will solve all the problems.

Organizations must remember that data is not magically transformed into something useful only when it arrives in an

Excel spreadsheet or database. Several forces, such as human error, automated misconfigurations, siloed processes, and unclear ownership, collaborate to introduce errors all the time. Recognizing and understanding these forces is the first defense against GIGO, allowing you to identify red flags before they turn into large-scale disasters.

As you advance in your understanding of how data can deceive, remember the main lesson of this chapter: *no spreadsheet formula or sophisticated algorithm can save data that was already flawed.* Garbage in really means garbage out, and no amount of reformatting or modeling can change this basic reality. The only way to overcome it is to ensure, as far as possible, that the data you use reflects a genuine and reliable view of the world you are trying to analyze.

In the next chapter, we'll see that even when the data itself is accurate, people can still go astray, especially by confusing *correlation with causation.* If GIGO weakens the basis of decision-making, confusing one pattern with another distorts our understanding of the real forces at work.

CHAPTER 3

CORRELATION VS. CAUSATION

> *One of the first things taught in introductory statistics textbooks is that correlation is not causation. It is also one of the first things forgotten.*
>
> — THOMAS SOWELL

Human beings have an innate desire to find patterns in everything around us. This propensity to seek out cause-and-effect narratives goes back to our most primitive instincts. For early humans, identifying correlations such as "storm clouds gather before thunder" or "certain plants cause disease" was a matter of survival. Learning these associations helped us prepare for threats or exploit opportunities.

Over generations, our brains have been programmed to quickly detect patterns and assume that they point to a direct causality. "If A happens to B, then A must be leading to B, right?" In evolutionary terms, an occasional false positive was less damaging than missing a genuine cause.

But for modern decision-making, this idea can be more dangerous. A marketing team may notice that increased social media conversations coincide with increased sales, concluding that more tweets "cause" increased revenue. A healthcare start-up might observe that patients who use a particular app have better health outcomes, rushing to claim that the app is the driving force behind their well-being.

However, these simplistic leaps often ignore other realities: a confounding factor may be driving both trends, or we may have reversed the direction of the arrow, or it may simply be a coincidence in the data.

We love clear, linear stories, especially those that we can easily implement as action items. A cause-and-effect story is simpler to convey in a meeting: "We've discovered that variable X drives variable Y, so let's reinforce X". It's incisive, conclusive, and easy to share.

The media also prefer headlines that put the finishing touches on complex issues. A headline that says, "High coffee intake is associated with a lower risk of heart disease," can be incorrectly rephrased as "Coffee prevents heart disease."

The subtle change from "associated" to "prevents" can shape public perception. Before you know it, consumers are buying coffee in large quantities, convinced that they are taking a proactive health measure. Meanwhile, the actual research may have shown only an association; perhaps people with healthier diets also drink coffee or have other, more important habits.

None of this means that we should ignore the patterns. Correlation can, in fact, be a very good clue. But we should be careful: behind every correlation, there may be several alternative explanations, and finding the genuine cause and effect is often a much more complex quest.

This chapter investigates why correlation often leads us to the wrong conclusions, how we can identify the difference between correlation and causation, and what it means to deal with correlated variables responsibly. If the previous chapters presented how numbers can give a misleading air of certainty or can be compromised from the outset, this chapter turns the lens on the process of interpretation itself: How do we move from observing a pattern to explaining it? By the end, you should be able to look at a pretty graph or an impressive statistic and think: "Interesting correlation, but what's really going on under the surface?"

DEFINITION OF CORRELATION (AND ITS LIMITS)

Correlation refers to a statistical relationship between two variables in which they move together, either directly (when one goes up, the other goes up) or inversely (when one goes up, the other goes down).

Mathematically, correlation coefficients range from -1.0 (perfect negative correlation) to +1.0 (perfect positive correlation), where 0 indicates that there is no linear relationship. For example, if ice cream sales and temperature have a correlation coefficient of +0.85, this suggests a strong positive relationship: as the temperature rises, so do ice cream sales.

It's a powerful concept in data analysis because it quickly tells us when two measures fluctuate together. You'll see correlation analysis in everything from marketing experiments to operational optimizations. A restaurant chain might notice a correlation between the number of staff available and average customer satisfaction scores, or a technology platform might find a correlation between the frequency of push notifications and user logins.

However, a high correlation coefficient is not inherently significant, apart from telling us that the two variables move in sync or nearly so. It doesn't explain *why* they move together. This is where many analyses stumble. Without further investigation, it's easy to assume a direct chain: Variable A leads to result B. But the coefficient itself says nothing about the reasons.

Spurious Correlations

In the era of big data, the phenomenon of spurious correlations has become increasingly visible. As massive data sets contain thousands (or millions) of variables, purely random alignments can appear as strong correlations. For example, it is possible to find a correlation between the number of films released by a particular actor in a year and changes in global weather patterns in that same year. The two variables have no logical connection, but if you research enough data, random pairs with a high correlation will inevitably emerge.

These spurious correlations highlight the difference between *coincidence* and causality. The more variables you measure, the more coincidences you will discover, some of which may show a robust statistical relationship. If you're not careful, you can draw big conclusions from random noise.

The comical aspect of these bizarre "links" hides a serious problem: entire companies can chase a supposed correlation in their huge data records, invest millions, and later discover that it is pure chance.

Non-linear Relationships

Another limitation of correlation is that it measures linear relationships by default. Suppose two variables have a curvilinear relationship (like an inverted U shape); they move together at first, but then diverge. A simple correlation coefficient can mask this relationship, showing a weak or even zero correlation.

You may incorrectly conclude that there is no connection because you used the wrong tool or never checked the curvature of the scatterplot. In other words, correlation alone can be a very blunt instrument when relationships are more complex than a straight line.

THE THREE MAIN TYPES OF FALSE CAUSATION

When two variables increase or decrease together, it's tempting to conclude that one must be driving the other. In reality, as we've seen, many correlations turn out to be misleading, leading us down the wrong path if we ignore the complexities beneath the surface.

This is where false causality comes into play, scenarios in which an apparently direct link between two variables disguises other, more complex forces at work. The following sections detail the three main types of false causality (confounding factors, reverse causality, and coincidental correlation), illustrating how each can derail sound strategic analysis and decisions.

Confounding Factors

Even when a correlation is real, we need to ask whether a third, invisible variable—a *confounding* factor—is manipulating both sides of the equation. Confounding factors are the real cause, while the two observed variables only respond in parallel.

Imagine a scenario in which employees who drink more coffee at work also submit more project proposals. It's easy to come to the conclusion that caffeine increases creativity, but there may be a confounding factor at play: perhaps motivated type A personalities drink coffee and propose bold ideas. The real cause is an innate drive to stand out; coffee drinking is just a passenger along for the ride.

These hidden variables appear in social science research, health outcomes, and market trends. In general, they go unnoticed if analysts don't measure them or even consider them relevant. A marketing analysis can link email campaigns to higher sales, ignoring the fact that the company aired a well-received TV commercial at the same time. In this case, the commercial is the real impetus behind the increase in sales; the email campaign is simply riding the same wave of consumer enthusiasm.

How Confounding Factors Distort Analysis

Confounding factors can amplify or mask perceived correlations. In the coffee example, the correlation may appear to be a clear one-to-one effect, but if the confounding factor works differently in the subgroups, the overall number may distort reality. For example, the confounding factor could amplify the effect in one department and attenuate it in another, causing a misleading aggregate result.

In research environments, techniques such as *multivariate regression* or *randomized controlled studies* can identify and take into account these third factors. However, many business analyses never reach this level of rigor. Under deadline pressure, analysts see an eye-catching correlation and rush to draft a strategic memo. Only later do they realize that they missed the real determining factor, brand reputation, seasonality, or some intangible factor that nobody thought to measure. When this happens, companies are left adrift, searching for illusions.

Reverse Causality

Another major pitfall is *reverse causality*, where you look at two linked variables and assume that one drives the other, only to discover that the relationship is reversed. This is especially problematic when the direction of causality is not obvious at first glance.

- **Advertising and sales:** A strong correlation between advertising spending and increased sales may seem like proof that ads increase revenue. But it may be that strong sales give the company more budget to spend on advertising, reversing the assumed direction.

- **Employee training and performance:** The correlation shows that employees with higher performance scores also receive more hours of training. Does training raise performance, or do the most outstanding employees seek (or receive) additional training? Or do managers channel their best employees into specialized programs, further enhancing the skills they already have?

Why We Don't Realize Reverse Causality

We often ignore reverse causality because we impose a quick narrative when a correlation is detected. It's cognitively simpler to say, "Variable A leads to result B," than to consider a complex loop. Furthermore, most analysis tools only calculate the strength of the relationship, not the direction. A correlation of +0.70 between two variables only tells us that they move together, not that one drives the other.

Time constraints in daily organizational life exacerbate this oversight. People want straightforward answers: "What do we do next?" If the data shows a convincing correlation, it is tempting to conclude that it is a straightforward cause-and-effect story. *Evaluating time series data, running controlled tests, or gathering deeper context* can be time-consuming, and without an explicit incentive to dig deeper, reverse causality goes undetected.

Coincidental Correlation

While confounding factors and reverse causality are classic forms of misleading correlation, the broader issue is often *coincidence* in a complex world. Modern markets, social behaviours, and organizational processes have a multitude of moving parts, so it is surprisingly easy to find two trends that move together for reasons unrelated to direct causality.

In large data sets, random alignments can appear highly significant. A company's morale score can have a suspicious relationship with international currency fluctuations, leading analysts to invent elaborate theories about economic optimism. But in fact, the correlation may be nothing more than a mathematical coincidence.

Simplistic Narratives Versus Systemic Realities

Organizations thrive on clear, linear stories. When faced with a correlation, decision-makers often yearn for a simple action: "If X drives Y, let's scale up X". However, the real world rarely cooperates with these simple outlines.

A correlation can reflect overlapping influences from several variables, some of which have not even been measured by the analyst. Condition X may only help in certain market conditions while overshadowing larger factors at other times.

Simplistic narratives born of coincidental correlations can be dangerously misleading. In fact, "taming" complexity requires *patience, additional data, and a willingness to recognize that immediate answers can be illusory.*

DISTINGUISHING CORRELATION FROM CAUSATION

Having established how correlation can tempt us, let's look at some ways of dealing with it responsibly. Although a single correlation statistic rarely proves anything, there are strategies to strengthen or weaken a hypothesis about causality.

Temporality and Time Series Analysis

One of the first checks is temporality: for A to cause B, A must precede B in time. If you're dealing with monthly data, do changes in A consistently occur before changes in B? If not, you may be dealing with reverse causality or a purely coincidental relationship. Time series data, where each variable is tracked at successive intervals, can reveal lag effects (perhaps A precedes B by a month) or show that B changes first, reversing your initial assumption.

Time series analysis can still be confusing if the variables are cyclical or if there are several lags at play. However, it is a direct improvement on the correlation of a single snapshot that groups all the data points together without considering their chronological order.

Controlled Experiments

A gold standard for establishing causality is the randomized controlled trial (RCT): randomly assign subjects (customers, employees, etc.) to two or more groups, apply different treatments, and measure the results. If one group receives a certain "treatment" (such as a new marketing tactic or product feature) and the other does not, and you follow the results over time, you can be more certain that the differences are due to the treatment and not a confounding variable.

Commercial contexts don't always allow for perfect RCTs, but many companies run *A/B tests* that have the same fundamental objective. For example, an e-commerce site might test two versions of a homepage to see which one generates more conversions. Randomly assigning visitors to each version helps reduce confounding factors since, in theory, each group is statistically similar. The line of cause and effect becomes clearer if the only difference is the design of the homepage.

Statistical Controls

When experiments are not feasible, statistical controls in observational studies can identify possible confounding factors. Techniques such as *multiple regression or propensity score matching* allow analysts to hold certain variables constant while examining the effect of another.

For example, you could measure employee coffee consumption and project proposals while controlling for job title, years of experience, and personality type. Although these methods don't guarantee perfect isolation of cause and effect, they can substantially reduce the risk of confounding factors getting in the way of your results. The key is thoroughness: the more relevant control variables you include, the more robust your analysis will be, provided you have sufficient data and well-specified models.

Triangulation With Various Data Sources

Another strategy is triangulation: collecting data from several independent sources or from different study projects.

If the same correlation appears in several data sets or after controlling for known variables, the case for causality is strengthened, but remember that this is not a guarantee.

However, consistency in different contexts is a strong sign. If, for example, you suspect that a particular marketing channel drives brand awareness, you can analyze both internal metrics (campaign performance) and external data (independent consumer surveys). If the correlation appears in both and stands up to scrutiny, your confidence in a cause-and-effect relationship may increase.

Observing Dose-Response Patterns

Another hallmark of a causal link is a dose-response relationship: as the "dose" of one variable intensifies, the "response" in the other variable grows accordingly. Suppose you monitor your marketing spend and the leads you generate. If doubling spending consistently doubles or substantially increases leads (over various periods or product lines), this is a stronger indication of a causal effect.

On the other hand, if the correlation remains sporadic or disappears after you pass a certain threshold, you may be looking at a more complex dynamic or a confounding factor. Although not infallible, consistent dose-response behavior generally reinforces the plausibility of causality, as random coincidences tend not to scale so predictably.

WHEN CORRELATION IS STILL USEFUL

After going through the countless ways in which correlation can be misleading, it's easy to become *overly cynical.*

However, the truth is that correlation still has its value, as long as we understand its limitations. Not every correlation mistaken for causation leads to terrible results, and sometimes, even a flawed assumption can point us in a direction worth exploring.

Harmless Associations Versus Dangerous Assumptions

- **Low-risk scenario:** A social media manager notices that posting at 3 p.m. is related to higher engagement. He assumes that 3 p.m. is the "peak engagement time" and continues to schedule posts at that time. Even if the real cause is the type of content and not the time of publication, the potential damage is minimal; at worst, the company misses out on an even more ideal window.
- **High-risk scenario:** A pharmaceutical start-up sees a correlation between a new compound and a lower incidence of a certain disease. Interpreting this as proof of efficacy, it launches expensive clinical trials or rushes the product to market. If it turns out that the real determining factor was a confounding demographic factor or a mere coincidence, they risk suffering huge financial losses and, more importantly, jeopardizing patient safety.

The key is to recognize the degree of *importance of* a given decision and how rigorously you need to test the correlation. In lower-risk situations, a small oversight can mean only minor inefficiencies or missed opportunities. However, if reversing a decision is costly or impossible, additional scrutiny is essential before acting on a supposed cause-and-effect relationship.

Generating Hypotheses and Early Warnings

In addition to managing risks, correlations can serve as *valuable clues*. In areas such as finance or operations, correlated variables can guide predictive models if used with caution. If you observe, for example, that employee satisfaction consistently moves in tandem with retention rates, you have a convincing indicator to dig into. This correlation alone is not a final verdict; it's just an invitation to investigate, test, and confirm or refute the role of employee happiness as a genuine driver of retention.

Correlations also help to *generate hypotheses*. Detecting an unexpected positive correlation between a specific marketing channel and high-quality leads can lead to targeted research: perhaps that channel is aligned with seasonal trends or reaches a particularly receptive niche audience. Although the correlation itself doesn't prove why the channel works, it does signal an area for further analysis or a controlled experiment.

In this sense, correlation is not the finish line but the *starting signal* for rigorous investigation. By keeping the risks of each decision in mind and using correlation as a guide (rather than conclusive evidence), you can take advantage of these statistical patterns without succumbing to the pitfalls of false causality.

FINAL THOUGHTS

Correlations appear at a rapid pace in modern analytics, emerging from machine learning, real-time dashboards, or even casual explorations in a spreadsheet. The sheer volume of measurable variables only increases the risk of stumbling across spurious patterns and mistaking coincidence for causation. Ultimately, the message is twofold:

1. *Correlation is a clue, not a conclusion.* It's the spark that says: "Here's a pattern; maybe something is going on". But it never guarantees which variable drives the other or whether another force is really behind it all.
2. We have *methods* to deepen time series checks, controlled tests, statistical controls, and triangulation, but each of them requires diligence and a willingness to deal with complexity. When data-driven decisions rely exclusively on attractive correlations, the organization runs the risk of oversimplifying complex phenomena and making costly mistakes.

We need to remember that the pitfalls of correlation go far beyond trivial matters; major strategic choices, political decisions, and multi-million dollar product launches can be undone by the assumption that "A causes B" simply because two lines move in sync. Failure to confirm causality can trigger a cascade of wasted resources, damaged credibility, or misguided corporate direction.

At the same time, a healthy dose of *intellectual humility* is indispensable. Seeing a strong correlation and saying, "That could be important; let's investigate it," is usually the most sensible course of action. This mix of curiosity and skepticism avoids investing in illusions and can also stimulate more creative thinking when it comes to discovering hidden factors or verifying time sequences. Even solid data can lead to erroneous conclusions when the story is more complicated than a single cause.

Remember that data rarely reveals its secrets as simple, linear cause-and-effect narratives. Accepting ambiguity is an important part of analyzing data. And in the next chapter, we'll look at how *overfitting* can create whole new illusions, causing us to see patterns that don't really exist. This new topic will reinforce our discussions that no matter how impressive the numbers look, they still require careful thinking and a willingness to question our first impressions.

CHAPTER 4

OVERFITTING AND FALSE PATTERNS

> *Humans are pattern-seeking story-telling animals, and we are quite adept at telling stories about patterns, whether they exist or not.*
>
> — MICHAEL SHERMER

BI often thrives on the promise that "the more data we analyze, the better our decisions will be". At first, this seems obvious: more variables, more sources, and more complex models should reveal hidden truths. However, in practice, taking complexity too far often produces *false patterns* that don't hold up under the pressures of the real world. This phenomenon, commonly known as *overfitting*, is one of the main causes of major analytical errors in both machine learning and human-led data interpretation.

Overfitting occurs when a model or analysis *fits the data too well*, capturing quirks and noise instead of legitimate signals. It's the equivalent, in the world of data, of hearing a random melody in the static of an untuned radio or identifying a face in an abstract blob of paint. The pattern seems convincing. It may even perfectly "explain" everything in the historical data set. But when new data comes in, or when the context changes, these supposed insights often fall apart.

In this chapter, we will explore the various ways in which overfitting and false patterns manifest themselves in organizational decision-making. We will investigate how the thirst for complexity can give rise to illusions and how both machines and humans fall into the same trap of "seeing" what is not really there.

We will also distinguish overfitting from the broader notion of "garbage data" and from illusions of accuracy or correlation (discussed in previous chapters), focusing here on the *mechanics* of capturing random noise and interpreting it as meaningful. Finally, we will consider practical strategies for recognizing and mitigating overfitting, ensuring that advanced analytics genuinely meet business goals rather than producing seductive but empty patterns.

WHAT IS OVERFITTING?

In simpler terms, overfitting occurs when a predictive model is so well adjusted to historical or training data that it hastily "learns" the noise (fluctuations or random errors) along with the actual data. As a result, it excels at describing *past* data but fails to predict *future* scenarios or adapt to *new* information. It's like a student who memorizes all the examples in the textbook but panics when faced with a slightly different test question.

When creating predictive tools, recommendation engines, or any data-driven model, the holy grail is *generalization*: the ability to deal with new information that wasn't part of the historical or training data set. Overfitting models fail to generalize well because they are effectively "reproducing" memorized things that have little to do with genuine causal relationships.

Overfitting doesn't require advanced machine learning. Even simple regression or clustering can collapse if analysts keep adding factors, cutting data, or "adjusting" the model until it explains everything, including the previous data. The result is a dangerously persuasive but empty solution.

In contrast to the previous chapter's focus on correlation versus causation, where we might mistake a mere association for a real driving force, overfitting is about capturing ephemeral patterns in historical data that don't hold up when conditions change.

While correlation errors often lead us to incorrectly state that "X causes Y", overfitting reflects a different trap: the creation of a model so adapted to past data (including its random peculiarities) that it cannot be generalized to new information.

Essentially, correlation traps confuse relationships, while overfitting traps confuse noise with genuine patterns, producing solutions that appear accurate but fall apart in real-world practice.

Why It Happens

Although the phenomenon of seeing false patterns does not require advanced algorithms, it is worth looking briefly at *how machine learning systems* overfit, given the prevalence of these tools in modern BI.

Models With Excessive Parameters

Neural networks and other machine learning models can have millions of parameters. This incredible capacity allows them to model virtually any pattern in the training data, including random noise. Without safeguards such as regularization (which penalizes complexity), these algorithms can produce near-perfect accuracy during training but fail drastically once deployed. For example, an AI system that "learns" every quirk of historical customer behavior can fail when consumer trends change or new products are launched.

Insufficient or Biased Training Data

Even a well-designed model can overfit if the dataset on which it was trained is too small or unrepresentative. The system ends up memorizing the training examples instead of learning generalized insights. Imagine creating a recommendation engine for an online store but training it mainly with data from a single region. The engine could work wonders for users in that region, but fail elsewhere because it has adapted too much to regional tastes that don't generalize to a wider audience.

Over-Training In Search Of Perfection

In search of incremental gains in accuracy, data scientists sometimes run the training for many iterations or keep adjusting the hyperparameters until the model matches every detail of the historical data. This approach generates diminishing returns in actual predictive performance. It's like rewriting every part of your code to deal with extreme cases that may never recur, while ignoring the broader functionality that really matters.

FALSE PATTERNS: SEEING WHAT ISN'T THERE

Pareidolia is the tendency to perceive meaningful images in random or ambiguous visual patterns, such as identifying a face in the craters of the moon (The general term for this would be apophenia, involving any type of information, such as auditory). A similar phenomenon occurs in data analysis (Gordon, 2024). We see shapes and trends where none actually exist. Overfitting is partly a computational phenomenon, but it is also fueled by the same human instinct that craves well-defined narratives and patterns.

Also, remember our aversion to ambiguity. While real data rarely offers perfect clarity, an overfitting solution can give the illusion of certainty: "Look, we've accounted for all the ups and downs of the last three years". This apparent precision seems comforting, especially for executives who want conclusive answers. Admitting that the data may be messy or that we can only identify partial truths can be more difficult. Thus, overfitting patterns fulfill an emotional need for completeness, even if they are misleading.

HOW OVERFITTING HURTS BUSINESS

Financial Forecasts

Financial analysts often want to explain the behavior of markets or asset prices as accurately as possible by sifting through a large amount of data, such as interest rates, commodity prices, exchange rates, and much more. It's easy for a hedge fund or a company's treasury department to create an overly complex model that perfectly "predicts" past crises and recoveries but fails to predict the next downturn. Each recession has unique catalysts, and each recovery presents new conditions. Memorizing the patterns of the last cycle can lead to overlooking different and critical triggers in the future.

Marketing

Companies want to be able to say: "This marketing channel contributed 30% of our new revenue; that channel contributed 25%," and so on. Marketing models usually try to distribute the credit between TV ads, social ads, and emails. As these models often incorporate dozens of parameters, overfitting is rampant. A skilled (or misguided) data scientist can keep adding complexities until the model explains everything from the campaign's historical data. Then, when a new product or competitor enters the scene, the model's crystal ball breaks.

Demand Forecasting and Stock Replenishment

Whether supplying grocery stores or electronics warehouses, the stakes are high for accurate forecasting. Some organizations adopt advanced forecasting solutions that incorporate large sets of external data, such as economic indices, weather data, and social media conversations. Over-adjustment can cause these systems to get caught up in random signals, such as an obscure factor that was only important in a particular year or region. The result is stock forecasts that may look excellent in historical tests but fail when a real change arises, such as a global event or a subtle shift in consumer preference.

Productivity and People Analysis

Overfitting can even lie in internal management dashboards. A company can track dozens of employee metrics such as meeting frequency, software usage times, and emails between teams to "detect productivity patterns". After creating a data model, one may find ephemeral correlations, such as meeting duration "explaining" code quality. The resulting policy changes might do nothing or even harm performance, because the model was capturing random coincidences unique to the training period rather than a real causal force.

RECOGNIZING WHEN A MODEL IS OVERFITTING

Just as the "garbage in, garbage out" principle alerts us to bad data, organizations need reliable ways of detecting overfitting before it wreaks havoc. Below are common warning signs and practical checks.

Technical Indicators

- **Validation on new data:** A gold standard in model development is split between training and testing, and *cross-validation*. For example, you segment your historical dataset, training the model on part of it and testing it on a separate "unseen" portion. If your model performs brilliantly on the training set but fails on the test set, this is a classic sign of overfitting. In trade setups, you can replicate this principle by asking: "Is the same pattern true on a different timeframe or in a different market?" If the correlation or model result does not persist in these subsets, it is likely to be ephemeral. If your model can handle variety, it is more likely to generalize.
- **Sudden drops in performance in live environments:** Another telling symptom of overfitting is strong performance during internal testing, followed by a sharp drop when the system goes live. The real world rarely replicates its perfect historical conditions. If your sophisticated forecasting tool or recommendation algorithm collapses under new circumstances, such as an unexpected holiday surge or a competitor's price change, overfitting is the prime suspect.

- **Unexplained complexity**: Overfitting solutions usually come packaged with an imposing set of parameters or variables. However, the people promoting them may not have a coherent explanation of the importance of these factors. If you ask, "Why does the local field hockey team's winning record predict our sales of jackets?" and the best answer is "because the data says it does", you're probably dealing with an overfitted model or an unsubstantiated correlation. Genuine insights usually come with plausible and relevant reasoning.
- **Hyper-focus on metrics**: Sometimes, an organization or data science team becomes obsessed with a specific metric, such as "maximize R-squared" or "minimize error in historical data". Without constraints, a model can pursue that metric to the detriment of real-world utility. This can lead to solutions that look mathematically beautiful but fail when confronted with new data. If you notice that a model is being evaluated primarily based on how well it fits old data rather than how well it can adapt to new data, this is a warning sign of overfitting.

Cultural and Procedural Pitfalls

Overfitting doesn't just develop because of analytical flaws; organizational factors can encourage it. If leadership demands absolute certainty, data teams may keep tweaking models to get perfect historical fits, unwittingly rewarding illusions. In environments without *feedback loops*, an attractive dashboard or graph can go unchallenged, especially if it promises clear and decisive answers.

Some executives also fall victim to the *"magic box" syndrome*, treating advanced analytics as unquestionable oracles instead of investigating how they arrived at their perfect results. Finally, relying on a single model for all important decisions increases the damage if that model is overfitted, especially if simpler baselines or alternatives are not used for comparison.

THE RIGHT BALANCE BETWEEN SIMPLICITY AND COMPLEXITY

Creating predictive models or analytical frameworks requires a delicate dance: too little complexity and you miss important things (underfitting); too much complexity and you start "learning" noise (overfitting). Understanding this balance helps organizations develop robust and adaptable solutions that capture legitimate insights without chasing every random fluctuation.

Avoiding the Twin Traps: Underfitting vs. Overfitting

Underfitting occurs when a model is too simplistic to capture important structures or patterns in the data. For example, applying a single linear trend to forecast a cyclical market leaves out many nuances, resulting in naive or incomplete forecasts. At the other end of the spectrum, as we have seen, overfitting arises when a model fixates on historical peculiarities, generating an illusion of perfect accuracy that quickly collapses when real-world conditions deviate from the past.

The ideal point is a model that is refined enough to reflect genuine signals, but not so elaborate that it "memorizes" irrelevant details. Achieving this balance usually requires iterative testing, domain expertise, and objective performance metrics that assess the model's adaptation to new data (we'll look at this in more detail in Chapter 11).

Adapting Complexity to the Context

The ideal simplicity or complexity always depends on the problem in question. A smaller-scale and relatively stable environment, such as team scheduling for a known workflow, may only need one basic method. On the other hand, global supply chain optimization, with constantly changing variables, such as currency fluctuations and logistical constraints, may require a set of sophisticated models.

The key is to avoid generalized assumptions such as "more data = better model" or "fewer variables = better". Real-world problems often require a context-driven process: experiment with various levels of model detail, apply performance checks on unseen data, and get feedback from technical and operational stakeholders.

Use Occam's Razor

A classic guideline is *Occam's Razor*: when two models achieve comparable results, choose the simpler one. Simpler models tend to generalize better because they don't chase every tiny fluctuation in the training data.

It is important to note that simplicity does not mean trivializing the problem. It means adding complexity only when each extra feature or parameter demonstrably increases predictive ability in out-of-sample tests.

Regularization techniques such as L1/L2 penalties or dropout in neural networks further reduce excess complexity by penalizing excessively convoluted internal structures. Early dropout stops the model training before it memorizes the historical dataset. In scenarios without machine learning, the same principle applies: keep an eye on validation performance, stopping refinement when improvements reach a plateau or degrade on new data.

Leveraging Domain Knowledge and Monitoring

Even the best statistical methods cannot fully replace domain knowledge. If a retail analyst knows that sales of winter coats depend on the vacation season or the average temperature, they are more likely to identify spurious variables (such as local sports victories) and challenge unlikely "findings". Encouraging collaboration between data scientists and subject matter experts reduces the chances of adopting noise-driven models instead of real-world logic.

What's more, no model remains valid forever. As consumer preferences change, new competitors enter the market, or economic factors fluctuate, a previously robust model can become overfitted. Periodic updates to the model help keep the analysis grounded in current realities. By retraining with new data, reviewing assumptions, and adjusting parameters, you avoid clinging to outdated insights that no longer apply.

FINAL THOUGHTS

Remember, just as with false causation, not every overfitting conclusion leads to catastrophe; much depends on the possible risks. In low-risk cases, such as optimizing social media posts, the downside is usually a slight inefficiency. However, when a telecommunications company or a multinational bank makes multimillion-dollar bets on a "perfect" growth forecast derived from over-adjusted perceptions, the outcome can be ruinous if real-world conditions diverge from this perfectly memorized script. The higher the cost of being wrong, the more rigorously you must test and validate your models beyond historical data.

Overfitting reflects a refusal to accept the inherent messiness of reality. No model can predict all the twists and turns in an unpredictable world; striving for near-total accuracy often means that we only memorize the past to the detriment of adapting to the future. Ironically, recognizing that some fluctuations will remain unexplained can promote more resilient analysis. When data teams accept a certain level of noise, they can focus on extracting meaningful and robust signals that endure under varying conditions.

Resilient data cultures also treat analysis as an *iterative process*. They launch models with the understanding that the results are approximate and then continually feed real-world performance metrics and observations into the next update cycle. Overfitting is less likely to persist because each iteration of the model must be proven in constantly changing environments rather than resting on a single triumph of retrospective "perfection".

Another safeguard is to *communicate uncertainty explicitly*. Instead of presenting a forecast with a single marker, offer confidence intervals or scenario ranges that invite nuanced discussions about "best, worst, and most likely" outcomes. This habit combats the gravitational pull of overfitting, reminding stakeholders that the future can deviate from even the most elegant historical fit.

Overfitting is seductive precisely because it seems to reveal all the nuances of previous data, a reassuring cover of precision. In practice, it captures ephemeral peculiarities that may disappear when tomorrow doesn't mirror yesterday. Importantly, overfitting is not limited to machine learning algorithms; *human analysts can be just as prone to forcing complexity into ambiguous trends* if they are driven by prejudice or a desire for certainty.

Despite these pitfalls, the solutions do not require abandoning complexity or big data. Instead, they rely on careful validation (such as cross-validation), domain expertise, and acceptance of imperfection. Healthy organizational cultures, in which "perfect fits" are questioned rather than revered, help prevent illusions from guiding strategic decisions.

By recognizing the difference between genuine signals and transient noise, we develop the humility and discipline to create BI systems that adapt and resist rather than cling to patterns that disintegrate under the pressure of the real world.

Even if your model isn't overfitted, summary statistics can be dangerously misleading. In the next chapter, we'll examine the *dangers of relying on averages*, exposing how a single "typical" number can hide enormous variability, distort interpretations, and fuel bad decisions. The illusions of BI don't end with overfitting or correlation errors; they extend to the subtle ways in which even apparently simple metrics can distort our view of reality.

CHAPTER 5

THE DANGER OF AVERAGES

> *Average is always a safe choice, and it is the most dangerous choice you can make.*
>
> — ERWIN RAPHAEL MCMANUS

Ask most people for a quick summary of a set of data—such as company revenue, customer satisfaction, or even national income—and they will usually quote an average. We learn from an early age that the average (usually the arithmetic mean) is a handy shortcut for encapsulating a set of numbers into a single, easy-to-digest value.

"The average is 10, so we must be doing well!" This clarity aligns well with the fact that our minds crave definitive answers. If you track daily website visits, you can say, "We receive an average of 10,000 visits a day," and everyone nods, believing they understand your website's traffic pattern. In the same way, a financial director can declare, "On average, our profit margin is 12%", and this figure becomes shorthand for the entire financial health of the company.

We want these summaries because they reduce complexity. The alternative, examining the entire distribution—requires more time and explanation. But comfort can be misleading: it's one thing to know an average, but quite another to know how that average was formed. If your web traffic fluctuates a lot (2,000 visitors on Monday, 18,000 on Tuesday, etc.), an average of 10,000 may be mathematically accurate, but it's not useful from an operational point of view.

Historically, societies have used concepts similar to the average for centuries (such as "average" height and "average" life expectancy) to assess population trends. Over time, these concepts have been institutionalized from financial statements to official government statistics. The practice made sense in an era without great computing power: averages were a practical way of summarizing large groups quickly. Now, ironically, we have powerful tools that can deal with details at the distribution level, but many organizations still cling to the average as the main representation of a data set.

However, as we shall see, no single summary can capture the full shape of a distribution. The average can be dragged down by outliers, while the median can hide pockets of extreme values. Even the seemingly harmless label "average" can lead us to oversimplify or ignore important nuances.

In this chapter, we will learn why averages can be misleading, illustrating how a single number can hide critical diversity in your data. We'll see how the different types of averages work, where they excel, and where they fail. We'll see how outliers, skewness, and the shape of the distribution can turn "mean-based" perceptions into illusions. In this way, you will understand the pitfalls of relying too much on a single metric for decision-making and gain practical methods for revealing the reality behind the numbers.

DIFFERENT TYPES OF AVERAGES (AND THEIR LIMITATIONS)

When people say "average", they are usually referring to the arithmetic mean. However, there are other measures of central tendency, each with its own peculiarities and pitfalls.

Mean: The Most Common (And Most Misleading?)

The arithmetic mean is calculated by adding up all the values and dividing by the number of data points. It is easy to calculate and widely recognized. However, it is also highly sensitive to outliers: a single massive value can drag the average up or down, overshadowing the rest of the data set.

- **Business example:** If a small marketing agency has five clients who pay approximately $5,000 each per project and one giant client who pays $100,000, the average client payment may appear to be more than $20,000, completely distorting the agency's "typical" revenue situation.

In such cases, the average can quickly lose its representativeness, painting an inflated or deflated picture of "typical" performance.

Median: More Robust But Potentially Blind

The median is the middle value when the data is sorted in ascending order. If there is an even number of points, you use the average of the two middle values. As it focuses on the midpoint, it is less sensitive to outliers. For many real-world distributions, such as housing prices or income, the median can be more insightful than the mean.

However, the median can ignore the shape of the distribution. If 49% of your data is clustered at one extreme and 49% at another, with only 2% in the middle, the median may suggest a midpoint that hardly represents the two main clusters.

Mode: Only a Small Slice of the Story

The mode is the value that occurs most frequently in a set of data. It is particularly useful for categorical data (for example, identifying the most common job title in a company). However, it is rarely used as a stand-alone measure for numerical data in business contexts. In asymmetric or continuous distributions, the mode may not even be well-defined or relevant. If you have a wide range of unique sales transaction values, the mode may be zero (if many transactions do not exist on certain days) or trivial.

No single average fits all data equally well. Each measure can hide or reveal different aspects of the pattern. Over-reliance on a single summary statistic (especially the mean) can distort conclusions about performance, risk, or trends.

WHEN AVERAGES HIDE CRITICAL INSIGHTS

Masking Variance and Outliers

One of the biggest dangers of relying on a single average is ignoring the dispersion of the data. Two sets of data can share the same average but differ enormously in terms of variation (how spread out the values are). If the variation is huge, the average is practically meaningless for operational decisions.

Suppose you run a chain of stores with an average weekly revenue of $50,000. Some stores may be making $100,000, while others are around $5,000. Just like the example of visitors to the website, sticking to $50,000 as the "typical store revenue" can lead to mistakes in expansions or budget decisions: high-performing stores may be anomalies, or low-performing ones may be in trouble.

Similarly, exceptions can push the average up or down, obscuring the experience of the majority. If a store reaches $200,000 during a special event, the chain's "average revenue" may increase, but this is not relevant to the normal performance of the other 49 stores.

The Long Tail Problem

Many real-world data sets, such as website traffic, e-commerce transactions, or product sales, have a long-tail distribution, meaning that a small percentage of customers or transactions account for a disproportionately large share of the total. In these scenarios, the average is dominated by the "head" of the distribution, overshadowing the long tail, where many smaller or infrequent events occur.

In e-commerce, for example, the top 5% of customers can generate half of the revenue, while the remaining 95% contribute the other half. Knowing the "average purchase amount" groups these distinct user segments together and can lead you to overlook important differences in user behavior. A marketing strategy based on the average buyer can be inadequate for both high spenders and occasional bargain seekers.

Aggregation Errors and Simpson's Paradox

When you aggregate data across subgroups, the average can produce misleading or even contradictory conclusions. Sometimes called a form of Simpson's Paradox, the aggregated average does not reflect the trends within each subgroup (Armstrong & Wattenberg, 2014).

Imagine you measure an overall improvement in sales conversion from 10% to 12% in a quarter. However, if you break it down by region, you may find that two areas rose from 8% to 15%, while another important region fell from 20% to 2%. The combined average "improvement" stems from disproportionate weighting or changes in each region's share of total sales. Relying solely on the overall figure of 12% diverts you from a crisis in that once-strong region.

The Myth of the "Average Customer"

Many marketing plans, product designs, and user experience decisions revolve around the "average customer". *This myth-*

ical being may not actually exist. Real customers have varied behaviors, preferences, and demographics. Designing for the "average user" can lead to features or services that nobody likes.

For example, the U.S. Air Force found that designing cockpits for the "average pilot" (based on average measurements of height, arm length, torso size, etc.) resulted in an uncomfortable fit for almost everyone. In trying to meet the average, they neglected the actual distribution of body dimensions among the majority (Rose, 2016).

In business, likewise, focusing on an "average user" can cause you to ignore crucial segments such as advanced users, loyal brand fans, or sporadic impulse buyers. The illusions promoted by this single average limit your ability to create targeted solutions.

BETTER ALTERNATIVES: USING DISTRIBUTIONS INSTEAD OF AVERAGES

Relying too much on a single average can obscure critical details. The antidote is distribution-focused analysis, a set of strategies that reveals how the data is actually distributed, where the anomalies are, and whether the subgroups differ significantly. The following are practical methods for going beyond the simplicity of the average and capturing a more nuanced view of your numbers.

Percentiles and Quartiles

A quick way to move beyond average-centered thinking is to look at percentiles or quartiles:

- **Percentiles:** They divide the data into parts. For example, the 10th percentile indicates the value below which 10% of observations fall, while the 90th percentile indicates where 90% fall below. Tracking the 90th percentile of customer support resolution time can show that, although its average is tolerable, a proportion of tickets consistently exceed any acceptable threshold.
- **Quartiles:** Dividing the data into four equal segments reveals where the middle 50% of the values (the interquartile range, or IQR) cluster. This can clarify whether the "average" really represents the majority of your data or whether it is distorted by a set of extreme values.

Example: A retailer may find that the top quartile of store revenues exceeds $70,000 monthly, while the bottom quartile receives less than $20,000. Grouping them into an "average" of $45,000 would miss two very different performance realities.

Standard Deviation and Variance

The standard deviation (SD) measures how much the numbers deviate from the average. A higher SD indicates greater variability, which can make the average less meaningful for decision-making.

For example, if the average shipping time is 5 days but the SD is 10, some packages may arrive overnight, while others may be weeks late. Emphasizing an "average of 5 days" misleads both customers and internal teams, who may assume a consistency that doesn't exist.

Closely related is the variance, the square of the SD, which serves a similar purpose by highlighting the dispersion of the data. Both measures tell you whether your data set is reasonably close to the average or very dispersed.

Visualizing Distributions

Box plots, histograms, and violin plots translate raw numbers into visuals that reveal the shape of the data, outliers, and groupings:

- **Histograms:** display how often data points fall into each interval, immediately signaling skewness or multiple peaks (bimodal distribution).
- **Box plots:** summarize the median, quartiles, and possible outliers in a compact graph.
- **Violin plots:** add more detail about the shape of the distribution, mixing elements of box plots and density plots.

Although these visualizations require a little more interpretation, they reveal insights that an isolated average could hide, such as whether different user groups dominate certain parts of a data set.

Retailers sometimes set prices or discount strategies based on "average customer demand". If demand is actually bimodal (with two peaks at different price sensitivities), the average-based approach can backfire. You can both alienate value buyers (by setting prices too high) and discourage premium buyers (by not offering a level of luxury).

Segmenting Data

In many organizations, a single average brings together different populations or product lines. By, for example, dividing an e-commerce user base by geographic region, purchase frequency, or device type, you avoid the pitfall of a single all-encompassing statistic.

The average revenue per user may be $50, but dividing users into high-value repeat buyers and occasional bargain hunters shows the average, variation, and distinct behaviors of each group. This segmentation helps to adapt marketing campaigns, product recommendations, or pricing strategies more effectively.

Combining Mean and Median

Sometimes, you want a single number to represent "typical" performance. Reporting the mean and median side by side can highlight how the data is distributed.

If the mean and median differ dramatically—say, a mean of $75,000 versus a median of $50,000—then the outliers with high salaries are skewing the mean upwards. Instantly, you see that the "average" data point is far below the mean, which indicates significant inequality or dispersion in the data set.

Range Tracking or Min-Max

Knowing the minimum and maximum of a data set can be a great discovery. If weekly sales range from $5,000 to $100,000, an "average" of $52,500 may be technically correct but not representative of either extreme. Observing these extremes generates productive questions: Are certain stores or periods vastly outperforming others? Are the anomalies linked to a specific time of year or location?

Weighted Averages

Occasionally, you need a consolidated metric, but a simple average can be misleading if the data set covers segments of very different sizes or importance. Weighted averages solve this problem by giving each subgroup a proportional weight.

For example, if 70% of your revenue comes from one region, that region should have a greater influence on the overall average. This technique prevents smaller segments with extreme values from excessively distorting a naive average.

Confidence Intervals

For more in-depth analysis or research, incorporating confidence intervals can show how certain (or uncertain) your estimate of the average is. If a 95% confidence interval for the average monthly spend is $45 to $55, you'll know that the "average of $50" has a margin of error of plus or minus $5. This extra layer clarifies that the number is an estimate, not an absolute truth.

A Holistic View

To go beyond the average, you need to be willing to spend more time on distribution, variability, and segmentation. Each of these techniques helps you escape the pitfalls of oversimplification, such as:

- Ignoring subgroups or exceptions that deviate from the average.
- Failing to notice multiple peaks or skewed distributions.
- Failing to notice tail risks or extreme values that could be decisive for an initiative.

Incorporating these methods into routine reporting and analysis promotes smarter decisions, reduces blind spots, and captures the reality that real-world data rarely conforms to a single, precise number.

RETHINKING THE MANAGEMENT AND REPORTING CULTURE

Switching from simple averages to a more distribution-focused analysis requires an organizational change as well as a technical one. Many companies have entrenched practices of displaying a handful of KPI averages on monthly dashboards, reinforcing a culture that ignores the real diversity and variability in their data. A better approach requires:

- **Distribution-based KPIs:** To deal with the "danger of averages", you can expand your repertoire of KPIs. Instead of "average time to first response", report the

90th percentile time or the proportion of requests resolved within a certain threshold. Instead of "average revenue per user", track how many users spend less than $10, between $10 and $50, and over $50. These distribution measures highlight both typical performance and extreme cases, reducing blind spots.

- **Contextualization of metrics:** Just as we learned that correlation does not automatically imply causation or that more complexity does not mean better models, we must also realize that one metric, such as the mean or median, cannot sum up everything. High-level metrics must be adapted to the reality of each department, ensuring that they take into account factors such as seasonality, customer segments, and evolving market conditions.
- **Data literacy and critical thinking:** Moving away from metrics based on singular averages involves some cultural and educational effort. Employees and stakeholders need to feel comfortable interpreting quartiles, variability, and outliers. Workshops, internal guides, or quick "data interpretation tips" can empower teams to question reports based solely on averages. Encouraging teams to ask questions such as "What is the range or distribution behind this average?" or "Are there outliers or multiple groups of data?" promotes a more critical and differentiated data culture.
- **Accountability in analysis:** Sometimes, analysts themselves use the average as a standard because it is quick and widely accepted. Encouraging full exploration with questions like "Show me the

distribution too" helps ensure that no hidden subgroups or extremes are overlooked. Over time, this responsibility can become an organizational norm: important decisions or announcements rarely depend on a single average but instead make reference to several measures that capture the shape of the data.
- **Realistic communication rather than storytelling:** Organizations generally value data storytelling, which can be beneficial for engaging stakeholders. However, focusing on a single average to achieve a clear and compelling narrative can be counterproductive. The best stories can be those that acknowledge complexity, showing how the average can be misleading while explaining the distribution patterns that really drive strategy and earn long-term trust.

When organizations have incorporated these practices, they avoid the pitfalls of average-centric reporting, cultivate a more questioning data culture, and ultimately produce insights that better align with the messy, ever-changing reality of everyday business.

FINAL THOUGHTS

Averages have an enduring appeal: they are easy to calculate, simple to communicate, and widely accepted as a measure of "typical" performance or behavior. But, as this chapter highlights, that simplicity comes with risks. The mean, median, or any other summary can hide a great deal of variation, obscure outliers, and distort the way we interpret data. In an increasingly data-driven business world, the danger of over-reliance on one number, especially the average, is real.

When leaders limit themselves to average-based perceptions, they often miss critical segments, misjudge risks, or design products that serve no one well. Shifting the organizational mindset toward distribution awareness, whether through percentiles, variance, segmentation, or advanced metrics, opens the door to more accurate, equitable, and successful decisions.

In short, recognizing the dangers of averages is not an attack on the concept itself; it's an invitation to look beyond the single number and into the deeper stories hidden in the data. While previous chapters have examined the illusions of inaccurate data or correlation errors, and we've discussed the dangers of overfitting, averages can be a subtle but equally potent culprit. By *adopting distribution-centric analysis*, we take an important step toward harnessing the true power of data, avoiding the simplistic trap of "on average, everything looks fine".

However, even the most nuanced metrics can be hampered by the way they are presented. In the next chapter, we'll explore *dashboards and deception*, discovering how visual design choices can easily distort or clarify our understanding of the truth.

CHAPTER 6

DASHBOARDS AND DECEPTION

> *A brain scan cannot interpret itself and neither can a data dashboard in education.*
>
> — ANDY HARGREAVES

In a world full of numbers and statistics, visual dashboards have become the ideal way to turn data into something that managers, executives, and even the general public can understand quickly. A well-designed dashboard can highlight trends, showcase achievements, and stimulate timely decisions. It seems like the perfect combination of art and analysis—a streamlined interface that captures everything at a glance.

However, this tool brings with it the capacity to deceive, whether intentionally or not. Dashboards can deceive our eyes by altering scales, omitting some data points, or employing sneaky visuals. Even small design elements, such as color schemes or how we label axes, can have radical impacts on the conclusions viewers will make. When a single form of graph is enough to influence high-level strategies or investments, the margin for deception (or error) is dangerously wide.

This chapter explores the various forms of dashboard deception, from innocently distorted bar charts to carefully selected data stories that obscure more than they reveal. While previous chapters have addressed pitfalls such as over-reliance on a single statistic or false patterns, here we focus directly on how data is visually packaged and how this packaging can distort even accurate numbers.

In the end, you will understand how dashboards, although indispensable for BI, can become vehicles for disinformation. We will also describe ways to protect yourself against deception. Remember that a graph or dashboard can be just as misleading as a flawed dataset if it is designed (or read) without analysis.

WHY WE'RE DRAWN TO VISUAL DATA

Even before spreadsheets and BI tools, human beings communicated meaning through images: drawings of caves to map the terrain, sketches to design shelters, and constellations plotted in the night sky. Visuals compress complex ideas into something our brains can understand instantly. This is because visuals involve several cognitive systems at once: we perceive shapes, spatial relationships, colors, and contrasts, all in milliseconds. This multi-sensory consumption allows us to detect patterns quickly, which was a survival advantage long before it became a business analysis habit.

Today, this same instinct underpins the widespread appeal of dashboards. A bar or line graph isn't just easier to read than a spreadsheet; it looks more real. The brain treats a clear visual pattern as evidence, often more convincing than a verbal argument or a numerical table. This isn't just efficiency; it's a cognitive tendency. Visuals seem immediate, intuitive, and, above all, reliable.

The problem is that we reach conclusions faster than we question them. Studies show that *viewers can form a judgment about a design in less than five milliseconds* (Lindgaard et al., 2011). In those five milliseconds, few people pause to read the footnotes or question the axis scales. Our minds fill in the narrative without much resistance: Sales are growing. The strategy is working. There's no need for further discussion.

Design amplifies this. *Visual heuristics*, such as upward trends equating to success or bold colors representing significance, are built into the way we read dashboards (Lerouge et al., 2017). A graph doesn't need to lie to deceive; it just needs to omit details. A truncated y-axis, a selective time period, or a mislabeled category can lead the viewer to a confident but incorrect conclusion. And since graphs rarely come with a "margin of interpretation", even subtle visual decisions can carry enormous weight.

Storytelling increases risk. Modern dashboard culture values "data stories" that guide the audience to a clear conclusion. When done honestly, storytelling clarifies complexity; when done carelessly, it becomes propaganda. Emotional cues intensify the spell: a pulsating red heat map awakens urgency, while pastel blue tones project calm. Equally powerful is omission. A dashboard can trumpet user growth but ignore churn, painting a rosy picture while half of those new users quietly leave a month later. The narrative seems complete, but only because the uncomfortable data never appeared.

Then there's the *social layer*. In most organizations, dashboards are shared by people in positions of authority, such as senior analysts, department heads, and consultants. Challenging their design choices or questioning their visual framework can seem inappropriate, especially during high-pressure meetings. The stakes seem too high and the pace too fast to be stopped with skepticism. Thus, the visual is not questioned, and its message solidifies in the collective mindset.

To make matters worse, there is a lack of *visible provenance* for the data. Dashboards rarely reveal the origin of each number, how it was cleaned, or what assumptions underpin it. Without this context, graphs become substitutes for the truth. Even experienced professionals can treat them as neutral or "just the facts", when in reality they are the product of dozens of subjective decisions about what to show, how to show it, and what to leave out.

All this makes us believe that the panels are impartial, transparent, and purely informative. But behind each graphic, there are a series of judgments, design shortcuts, and narrative structuring. The more refined the panel, the more invisible these choices become.

Over time, this dynamic infiltrates the organizational culture. A kind of visual absolutism emerges: if the dashboard says the performance is good, it must be good. If it doesn't look good, there's no urgency. People stop asking whether the data has been selected fairly, whether the trend is statistically significant, or whether outliers have been conveniently removed. As dashboards become central to decision-making, their authority can eclipse the data itself.

This doesn't mean we should abandon dashboards, far from it. But it does mean that we need to approach them with the same critical lens that we apply to any analytical result. After all, what we see on a graph isn't the raw world—*it's someone's version of it*. And until we start treating visuals as arguments rather than answers, we will continue to be vulnerable to some of the most persuasive illusions that data can create.

COMMON TECHNIQUES OF DASHBOARD DECEPTION

Panels gain strength from their visual clarity, but that same clarity can be misused to steer opinions. Below are ten deceptive practices, each explained in detail, illustrated with concrete examples, and accompanied by signs that something is not right.

1. Manipulating the Axis

The axis of a graph is its visual backbone. Change it and you change the narrative.

- **How it works:** Designers truncate the Y axis so that it no longer starts at zero, or stretches the scale so that genuine volatility appears flat. This small modification can turn a 2% increase in revenue into a

towering skyscraper bar, or flatten a double-digit slide into a benign oscillation.
- **Example:** A bar chart of monthly sales starts at $950,000 instead of $0. February, at $1 million, looks twice as high as January's $970,000, even though the actual change is only 3%. When the same data is replotted from scratch, the "dramatic increase" practically disappears.
- **Spot it:** Check the axis minimums, look for uneven spacing between ticks, and compare similar charts - are the scales changing? If so, question why.

2. Careful Selection of Time Intervals

A trend depends entirely on where you start and end the line.

- **How it works:** Presenters highlight a slice of time that favors the metric, such as peak seasons, partial quarters, or the two weeks after a big promotion, while omitting periods that would dampen the story.
- **Example:** A SaaS company presents user growth from November to December, when a vacation promotion increased sign-ups by 15%. What they don't see is the 10% churn in October and the plateau in January. Investors come away convinced that the momentum is unstoppable.
- **Spot it:** Ask to see the previous 12- or 24-month trend. Sudden starting points at suspicious lows or abrupt end points just before a known drop are warning signs.

3. Redefining Metrics

Every metric, from "customer churn" to "conversion rate", depends on definitions. By adjusting these settings, dashboards can produce more favorable numbers.

- **How it works:** Before, a "daily active user" meant a login; now, it means any open push notification. Overnight, DAU increases by 40%. Unless stakeholders know about the change in definition, the increase seems real.
- **Example:** Decide that a "retained user" is anyone who logs in once in 90 days instead of 30 days. If viewers are not aware of these changes, they may applaud an "improvement" that is purely one of definition.
- **Spot it:** Read the footnotes, release notes, or KPI glossaries. If a metric increases without operational change, investigate the underlying formula.

4. Single-Source and Aggregation Bias

A data pipeline or a roll-up into different entities can hide contradictions.

- **How it works:** A marketing dashboard is based only on CRM, ignoring write-offs from the financial sector. Or a company-wide sales total merges regions with very different currencies and seasonal patterns, obscuring local trouble spots.

- **Example:** The dashboard shows "Global revenue up 8%". Behind the scenes, North America fell by 12%, but currency conversion from Asia increases the total. Aggregation masks a market at risk.
- **Spot it:** Look for corroboration from independent systems. If there are no cross-checks or if departmental metrics conflict, aggregation bias may be at play.

5. Visual Clutter and Obfuscation

Complexity itself can be a smokescreen.

- **How it works:** Overlapping lines, 3D explosions, or gradient pies overwhelm the eye. In the ensuing confusion, the presenter chooses a slice of the interpretation, while the audience is distracted.
- **Example:** A recipe share pie chart shows 15 slices in subtle blue tones; the legend is tiny. Stakeholders cannot discern that a single partner now controls 45% of sales.
- **Spot it:** Ask for a simplified version: fewer series, flat 2D visualization, or separate charts for different concepts. Resistance to simplification is revealing.

6. Color and Coding Tricks

Color encodes emotion long before the data reaches cognition.

- **How it works:** Bright greens highlight small gains; soft reds portray big losses. Or the same series is colored differently in successive graphs, making comparisons look new, rather than flat.
- **Example:** A heat map of regional performance uses high-saturation blue for "good" and light orange for "bad". At a glance, almost all the regions look strong, although half are below target.
- **Spot it:** Check for a consistent color legend. If the tones change between slides, or if the positive colors are more intense than the negative ones, pause and question.

7. Hiding Uncertainty

Confidence intervals are technical, so their omission often goes unnoticed.

- **How it works:** Predictions appear as clear trajectories, with no shaded error bands. Viewers assume accuracy and plan budgets accordingly.
- **Example:** A demand planning graph predicts 150,000 units per quarter for the coming year, a line drawn with precision. The model has an error of ±20%, but this range is invisible, which leads to purchasing block aggressive stockpiling.

- **Spot it:** Look for confidence bands, error bars, or sample sizes. In the absence of these elements, treat sharp future lines with skepticism.

8. Camouflaging Data Gaps

Silence about missing data simulates integrity.

- **How it works:** If a data feed fails, or a region is delayed, the dashboard will still display the (now incomplete) totals without warnings.
- **Example:** Europe's weekend transactions are published on Monday, but Sunday's "global revenue" updates show an alarming drop. The CFO reacts, unaware that a third of the revenue has not been uploaded.
- **Spot it:** Look for update timestamps or "last updated" notes. Unexpected delays, missing territories, or sudden corrections on Monday indicate camouflaged gaps.

9. Baseline and Comparison Games

Choose favorable references, and even mediocrity will seem incredible.

- **How it works:** A niche player compares its growth with a slow industry average rather than with direct competitors, or changes its baseline every quarter to mask long-term stagnation.

- **Example:** A telecommunications company reports ARPU growth in relation to an industry metric from five years ago. To its current peers, its ARPU is falling, but this comparison never appears.
- **Spot it:** Ask why a particular benchmark was chosen. If the baselines change from one slide to the next, insist on consistency.

10. Cumulative Illusions

Cumulative charts never go down, meaning they are perfect for hiding recent setbacks.

- **How it works:** A cumulative sign-up curve rises higher and higher, even after the monthly counts of new users stop. The dashboard title displays total users instead of declining additions.
- **Example:** Monthly net new users peak in March and then fall by 40% in June. The cumulative line still rises smoothly; only a month-by-month bar chart would expose the drop.
- **Spot it:** Ask for period-by-period visualizations along with the cumulative totals. A divergence between the two indicates hidden problems.

BEST PRACTICES FOR HONEST DASHBOARDS

Before dashboards can be enlightening, they have to be reliable. After exploring how visualizations can distort reality, the next step is to learn how to protect yourself against these pitfalls. The guidelines below describe the practical design principles and organizational habits that transform dashboards from potential propaganda into reliable decision aids.

1. **Use transparent scales and contexts:** Start axes at zero, unless a non-zero baseline really clarifies the details, and openly identifies any truncation ("The Y axis starts at $800k"). For time series visualizations, include enough history to show seasonality or long-term trend lines. If a narrow window is essential, provide an easy link or switch to the broader data so that viewers can see whether the highlighted slice is typical or exceptional.
2. **Define all metrics up front:** All metrics in a dashboard should be accompanied by a brief definition, even if it's a tooltip. If an "active user" or a "retained customer" is being measured, the user should know exactly what is considered eligible. Provide disclaimers for partial data or known problems, such as "Region C's data is updated weekly, others are updated daily". This promotes trust and clarifies any potential biases.
3. **Surface variability, not just averages:** Remember to use confidence intervals, error bars, or at least mention the margin of error for predictions. Show quartiles or percentiles in a bar next to an average. If a monthly average is shown, including a minimum-maximum range or a standard deviation, can reveal volatility. Even simple design elements, such as a shaded area around a line graph, can indicate that the future projection is uncertain, rather than set in stone.

4. **Enable search and source access:** Interactive dashboards allow users to click on a segment of the graph to see additional data or context. Providing these search capabilities allows users to validate or explore surprising numbers. The more a dashboard "hides" behind aggregated numbers, the more likely it is to be hiding complexity.
5. **Practice ethical data storytelling:** If a narrative structure is used, it should be based on transparency and not spin. Show contradictory or ambiguous data points alongside the main story. Resist the temptation to hide negative metrics or disclaimers. Ethical dashboards aim for clarity, even if the message is complex or not entirely flattering.
6. **Require peer review and cross-checks:** Before launch, forward dashboards to a second analyst or an adjacent department. Quick reviews of chart types, color schemes, and KPI definitions detect accidental (or deliberate) distortions. Cross-checking between teams also ensures that terminology (such as "active user") has the same meaning throughout the organization.
7. **Verify numbers based on real-world observation:** Periodically verify the dashboard's claims with field checks or sample audits. If the dashboard indicates 10000 sign-ups, but onboarding records only 2000 new customers investigate. Comparing digital readings with physical reality keeps data quality and trust intact.
8. **Align incentives with accuracy:** Reward teams for revealing early warning signs, not just for showing upward trends. Celebrating sincerity turns

dashboards into tools for continuous improvement rather than polished propaganda, thus reducing the temptation to create images.

Adopting these practices turns the dashboard into a reliable lens of reality, eliminating design tricks, hidden assumptions, and selective narratives, so that decision-makers see the data as it really is.

FINAL THOUGHTS

All of this boils down to cultivating a culture of critical thinking. Every team should be trained to instinctively ask: "How is this metric defined?" "Could the scale be masking small but important changes?" "What does the long-term trend look like?" When these questions become routine and non-confrontational, dashboards evolve from shiny slideware into genuine instruments of discovery.

Encouraging scrutiny does more than avoid visual gimmicks; it creates a space for richer, more nuanced conversations. When people feel safe to challenge a graph, they also feel safe to propose alternative explanations, flag suspicious peaks, or highlight gaps in the data that merit new collection strategies. Over time, this habit turns dashboards into "living documents", interfaces that improve according to the questions users dare to ask.

An honest dashboard practice also reminds us that seeing is not the same as understanding. The very speed that makes visuals attractive forces us to deliberately slow down, to note warnings, to revise assumptions as the information changes.

In doing so, we recover something that dashboards often steal from us: *time depth*. Static screenshots are instantaneous; business reality is continuous. A culture that normalizes follow-up questions naturally gravitates toward longitudinal displays, scenario breaks, and drill-downs, features that keep quick impressions linked to a deeper context.

A mindset that prioritizes the question highlights a subtle joy in analysis: uncertainty can be enlightening. A confidence band is not a design flaw; it is an honest admission that the future may be different from the present. A footnote about the lack of regional data is not an excuse; it is an invitation to strengthen data pipelines. When leaders applaud these revelations, teams are no longer afraid to reveal unpleasant truths. Accuracy and the humility that underpins it become shared assets.

Looking to the future, dashboards are just one layer in the architecture of persuasion. Behind each graph is the *metric itself*: how turnover, engagement, or productivity has been defined, broken down, and weighted. A flawless visualization can still be misleading if the underlying metrics are manipulated from the start.

In the next chapter, we'll talk about *manipulated metrics*, exploring how seemingly objective numbers are framed, stretched, or redesigned to suit a narrative long before they reach a graph. Just as we learned to question axes and color scales, we now need to examine the very parameters by which performance is judged.

CHAPTER 7

MANIPULATED METRICS

> *The numbers should speak for themselves, but they don't. Growth metrics are the misunderstood teenagers of the tech world with murky intentions.*
>
> — MOLLY NORRIS WALKER

In the previous chapters, we unraveled the layers of BI to expose a series of ever-deeper illusions: from "precise" decimals to flawed inputs, from the mirage of mere correlation to overly complex models, and from the sheen of polished dashboards to the false comfort of simple averages.

Each chapter showed how our well-intentioned efforts to tame data can, without us realizing it, create traps, channeling our attention into narratives that flatter rather than inform. These errors, however serious, share one curious thing in common: they still presume that the metrics themselves, those carefully counted and algorithmically processed numbers, are immutable offerings of objective truth.

In many situations throughout this book, we have seen that the numbers we choose to display, the formulas we employ to calculate them, the time windows we select, and even the decimal places we include or omit can distort reality toward a preferred narrative. This is not always the result of sloppy data or naïve analysts, but rather of conscious design decisions that turn reasonable measures into instruments of persuasion, self-interest, or pure performance theater.

This chapter confronts an even more disturbing reality: What happens when the measurement tools themselves become malleable? When a metric is no longer a neutral mirror for performance but clay to be sculpted into the shape of a desired story?

In the high-pressure environment of quarterly reviews, board meetings, and investor presentations, the desire to present "good" metrics can override caution and integrity. Sales figures can be outdated, definitions subtly reworded, or benchmarks discreetly altered—all in the name of keeping the needle moving upward. The numbers that once served as signals guiding strategy become instruments of persuasion, no different in principle from marketing texts or political manipulations.

This chapter, like all the others, is not intended just to arm you with a checklist of deceptive tactics, but to instill a deeply ingrained skepticism: the reflexive habit of asking: "How did this number come about?" before allowing that number to shape your most important decisions.

STATISTICS IS A CONSTRUCT

To understand manipulated metrics, we must start by recognizing that all statistics are a construct. A "customer satisfaction score" does not fluctuate in isolation, but is based on a survey instrument, a set of questions, a sampling method, and an aggregation rule. A "conversion rate" arises from a choice of numerator and denominator and a decision on the length of time.

At each stage, human judgment creeps in—some of it benign, some of it tinged with self-interest. When these judgments are used to shape the result rather than simply measure it, the metric ceases to be a neutral barometer and becomes an elaborate narrative.

Consider the simplest form of metrics manipulation: *framing*. Two companies can each add 1,000 new customers in a quarter, but one of them reports "20% month-on-month growth," while the other discreetly anchors its report in a completely different baseline, emphasizing "5% year-on-year improvement".

Both statements are technically true, but give totally different impressions. The first suggests explosive momentum; the second a steady effort. The choice of time window—daily, weekly, quarterly, or annually—becomes a lever by which excitement or complacency can be increased or decreased. At one board meeting, the story seems urgent and triumphant; at the next, measured and deliberate. Neither is inherently dishonest, but each is a product of selective emphasis.

The framing extends beyond time windows into the realm of *percentage versus absolute values*. When revenue jumps from $10 million to $12 million, the marketing team highlights a 20% increase, a headline number that jumps off the slide. However, when expenses rise from $9.5 million to $11 million, the finance department can hide an increase of 15.8% under the spotlight of the excess of a single million dollars.

Headlines prefer large percentages; lines of business prefer small dollar figures. The same raw data can be distorted to magnify successes and minimize setbacks.

GOODHART'S LAW AND PERFORMANCE FIXATION

If framing is subtle persuasion, then Goodhart's Law is the obvious distortion that follows: *"When a measure becomes a target, it ceases to be a good measure"* (Mattson et al., 2021). When a metric is linked to remuneration, promotion, or reputation, the incentive shifts from improving actual performance to optimizing the number itself.

In its mildest form, fixation on measurement resembles a sales team filling their pipeline with opportunities that will never convert, simply to brag about the volume. At worst, it can alter the very behavior that the metric was meant to guide. A customer service center evaluated solely on the basis of average service time will reward representatives who rush through calls, ignore complex issues, or even record fictitious "resolutions" to keep the numbers down. Metrics designed to measure efficiency ultimately lead to a poor customer experience.

In all sectors, Goodhart's Law hides behind the metrics that become performance contracts. In a distribution company, if warehouse managers are rewarded based on the speed with which orders are fulfilled, they can prioritize fast orders and indefinitely shelve slower, more complex ones. In software development, if team speed becomes the only indicator of productivity, programmers will inflate their story point estimates or divide tasks into trivial parts, artificially increasing speed without providing meaningful functionality. In education, when schools are evaluated solely based on average test scores, teachers "teach to the test", narrowing the curriculum and ignoring critical thinking skills that cannot be so easily quantified.

This phenomenon is not limited to line workers. Executives also learn to chase the metric rather than the mission. A marketing director obsessed with "impressions" may prioritize banner placements that generate eye-popping numbers but no engagement; a finance director obsessed with "EBITDA margin" may put off necessary capital expenditures that hurt short-term metrics at the expense of long-term health. In each case, the metric becomes an end in itself, rather than a means to making better decisions.

VANITY METRICS VERSUS ACTIONABLE METRICS

Vanity metrics are the other side of the coin. They are measures that look impressive on the surface, but have little operational value. When marketing teams boast of "1 million app downloads" or social media managers celebrate "50,000 followers", they evoke success, even if user engagement is negligible and churn rates skyrocket. *Vanity metrics have great visibility but little accountability.* They are easy to collect and difficult to dispute, which makes them seductive targets for slideshows and press releases.

The problem arises when these numbers supplant actionable metrics that actually measure value creation, such as retention rate, customer lifetime value, or net promoter score. A steady stream of downloads can hide an app that no one uses beyond the first day. A growing number of followers can hide a stagnant brand with little genuine advocacy.

Actionable metrics, on the other hand, require more in-depth analysis and are often more difficult to improve. They require an understanding of why customers stay, which characteristics promote loyalty, which channels generate quality opportunities, and where operational processes fail. They resist easy headline treatment.

However, when vanity metrics dominate executive dashboards, teams learn to produce slides devoid of substance, cultivating a culture of optics to the detriment of results. The dashboard becomes a funhouse mirror rather than a clear window to reality.

CHERRY PICKING: CREATING THE NARRATIVE

At the heart of manipulated metrics is the art of selection. Any large data set offers countless sub-segments and combinations. Analysts can segment by geographical area, customer level, product line, marketing channel, device type, and time zone; each segment produces its own story. By selecting just the window or segment that shows the desired trend, it is possible to assemble a mosaic of seemingly irrefutable evidence.

This practice can start innocently enough, with an analyst thinking: "Let me just check this region," and end up with a truncated narrative that ignores contradictory evidence. *The cherry picker's mantra is simple: focus on the most convenient points and discard the rest.*

Moreover, cherry picking doesn't just distort external audiences; it erodes the very feedback loops that drive improvement. When teams only see the slices that reinforce a success story, they lose sight of the underperforming segments where real problems lurk and miss opportunities to learn from failures.

Over time, this selective narrative breeds complacency and blinds decision-makers to emerging risks. Worse still, when stakeholders become aware of the practice—perhaps when they come across a report that contradicts the selected slice—they begin to doubt all the numbers, becoming skeptical that there might be another, less flattering version waiting just out of sight. In this way, selective selection not only misleads in the moment, but also undermines confidence in any metric in the future.

SMOOTHING AND MOVING AVERAGES: THE FANTASY OF STABILITY

Another favorite of metrics sculptors is the application of smoothing windows or moving averages to disguise true volatility. Instead of presenting raw figures period by period —monthly revenues, weekly churn rates, daily active users—

analysts replace them with moving averages of three, six, or even twelve months.

At first glance, this "cuts through the noise", but in practice, it turns sharp drops and fleeting peaks into a gentle upward slope that rarely deviates. A sudden 20% drop in registrations disappears when buried in a three-month average; an unexpected service failure dissolves at the bottom of a six-month trend line.

By selecting different smoothing windows for different KPIs —say an average of three months for sales growth, six months for customer satisfaction, and one year for retention —a presenter can create each graph to look perpetually healthy, even if the company suffers significant short-term pain.

These smoothed curves not only hide the exact timing and severity of problems, but also actively discourage stakeholders from asking "Why now?" since there is no obvious "downfall" to explain.

True transparency demands that, alongside any moving average visualization, the unsmoothed series be made available, either as a button on an interactive dashboard or as a small embedded graph, so that viewers can assess both signal and volatility.

SHIFTING BASELINES: MOVING THE GOALPOSTS

We've already discussed how insidious shifting baselines can be. Metrics rarely remain static; definitions can change from month to month or quarter to quarter. A company may announce that its "retention rate has risen from 60% to 65%", only to discreetly broaden the definition of "retained customer" to include anyone who logged in during the period, rather than those who made a purchase.

The result is a figure that appears to improve through operational excellence, when in reality, it is just redefined. These shifting baselines can be buried in footnotes (or omitted altogether), leaving stakeholders unaware that the metric they were basing them on has been subtly rewritten.

Sometimes the baseline change is a deliberate backtracking. A metric that previously measured an ambitious goal is lowered mid-quarter to ensure that the team "meets expectations".

When indicators become *internal weapons*, perverse incentives arise. If managers' bonuses depend on a particular indicator, they will look for every loophole they can find. In a factory, if downtime is penalized, teams can record minor stoppages as "planned maintenance" or "calibration", transferring real downtime to benign categories. In retail, if shrinkage (loss through theft or error) is measured as a percentage of sales, store managers can inflate sales through false discounts to increase the denominator, thus reducing the paper shrinkage rate. Nobody is falsifying the numerator; they are falsifying the whole formula.

Siloed definitions exacerbate this situation. Different teams often maintain their own versions of what should be common metrics. The sales department considers everything beyond a certain order size to be "new business", while the finance department considers renewals and upgrades to be new business if they are processed to a certain code. The customer success department classifies churn differently from accounting, which writes off an invoice that is 90 days overdue.

When these definitions are never reconciled, it becomes trivial for managers to choose the version of the metric that most favors their performance. Each department lives in its own metric reality, and the organization as a whole has no single truth.

EXTERNAL SPIN: MANIPULATION BEYOND THE ORGANIZATION

Manipulated metrics extend beyond the walls of the company and into the realm of external spin. Investor relations presentations, annual reports, and sustainability disclosures are all conducive to selective optimism. A company can proclaim a reduction in carbon emissions by communicating the intensity (emissions per unit of production) rather than the absolute values, conveniently hiding the absolute increases that occur when production rises.

Banks proudly announce improvements in their "risk-weighted asset" ratios without revealing that risk weightings have been redefined to favor certain asset classes. Regulators may receive a set of figures which, on the face of it, are acceptable, but which, underneath, conceal variable definitions.

Marketing departments, eager to dispel skepticism, often present these manipulated metrics in glossy graphs and without footnotes. A consumer goods company can claim a 30% improvement in recycling rates, without clarifying that the old baseline included only beverage packaging, while the new figure encompasses all types of packaging by widening the scope to include easier categories, the percentage increases. The narrative is convincing: sustainability heroes and increased recycling, but the reality is that nothing fundamental has changed. *Only the measurement has changed.*

In the world of public policy, where metrics can influence funding and votes, the manipulation of metrics takes on a political tinge. A municipal government can report crime rates using a threshold that excludes certain categories of nuisance calls, presenting a declining crime curve even as citizens' calls for help increase. A school district may measure the "graduation rate" by including students who transfer to alternative programs or GED courses, hiding a decline in students who complete the traditional diploma. Without standardized definitions and independent audits, these numbers become malleable narratives rather than reflections of reality.

TECHNICAL SAFEGUARDS AGAINST METRIC MANIPULATION

Tackling metric manipulation requires both technical safeguards and cultural countermeasures. From a technical point of view, the simplest step is to *establish immutable metric definitions*, ideally codified by a single authority, with version control to record any changes. Whenever the formula for "active user", "churn rate," or "operational uptime" is changed, the change should be logged, time-stamped, and communicated to all stakeholders.

Dashboards should display not only the current values, but also the version of the metric definition in use and the date of the *last update*. This transparency turns silent changes into visible events, reducing the temptation to introduce a new setting without warning.

Equally important is the introduction of *multi-metric scorecards*. No single indicator, however well defined, can capture the full complexity of performance. Balanced scorecards, which combine financial, customer, internal process, and learning metrics, help to avoid excessive fixation on a single measure. If revenue per user increases but the net promoter score decreases, the conflict between these metrics requires attention. When several independent indicators have to move together, the room for selective maneuver decreases.

Peer review and cross-functional audits are another powerful deterrent. Just as scientific journals insist on blind reviews, organizations should treat KPI proposals as drafts subject to scrutiny by teams that don't depend on the outcome. A new metric designed by marketing goes through the finance, legal, product, and customer success teams to get feedback. Each group has a different perspective, identifying potential gaps or unintended consequences.

In Chapter 11, we will look at a broader toolkit of technological and procedural mechanisms for safeguarding the integrity of metrics. These solutions will be based on the principles described here, showing how to incorporate metrics governance into continuous delivery pipelines and how to use anomaly detection to flag unexpected changes. You'll then have a clear roadmap for implementing these technical controls at scale, ensuring that your organization's KPIs remain reliable anchors rather than shifting sands.

FINAL THOUGHTS

By now, we've discovered the many ways in which numbers can be bent, stretched, and reframed. Decimal precision that seduces, flawed inputs that mislead, phantom patterns that disappear when exposed, averages that hide more than they reveal, and dashboards whose very design can lead us astray.

This chapter exposed the most fundamental manipulation of all: the act of choosing what to measure and how to measure it. A KPI is never neutral; it is built on decisions about definitions, time windows, denominators, smoothing techniques, and the important question of what, even within the data, is left out.

We should no longer accept any metric at face value. Instead, every number demands a moment's pause: Where did it come from? What does it actually capture, and what does it omit? Just as the previous chapters urged us to question decimal precision, investigate hidden assumptions, and look beyond averages, we should also treat every KPI as provisional. Each value should be accompanied by notes on data coverage, version history, known limitations, and any recent changes to the definition.

Technical safeguards: immutable metric definitions, version control, multi-metric scorecards, and cross-functional reviews make manipulation more difficult, but the real resilience lies in habitual scrutiny. When a surprising peak appears, the reflex should not be celebration, but investigation. When a drop appears, the impulse should not be defense, but curiosity.

Some people may fear that this level of questioning will lead to paralysis, that no number is "good enough" to be used. However, the alternative is much worse: unchallenged metrics become the fragile basis for critical decisions, only to crumble when reality refuses to align. Accepting the imperfections of metrics, recognizing their constructed nature, and establishing checks and balances do not impede decision-making; they make decisions more robust and adaptable.

Manipulated metrics are not just the domain of "bad actors". They arise naturally whenever performance measures gain inordinate influence, definitions become porous, and incentives reward polished numbers over genuine progress. Even the strictest processes and checklists can't fully protect against the peculiarities of human judgment - our eagerness to see success, our discomfort with uncertainty, and our habit of telling neat stories.

That's why, before we explore the real-world disasters and ethical minefields that manipulated metrics can create, we need to turn inwards. In the next chapter, we will examine the *cognitive biases* that silently shape the way we collect, interpret, and present data: confirmation bias, framing effects, the sunk cost fallacy, among others. By shining a light on these mental shortcuts, we equip ourselves to detect misleading metrics and resist the subtle impulses that lead us into the dark side of BI.

CHAPTER 8

COGNITIVE BIASES IN DATA ANALYSIS

> *Humans are not machines. They analyze information through the lenses of their experience, knowledge, and cognitive biases. All of it makes their perception, their unique viewpoint.*
>
> — NAVED ABDALI

So far, our expedition through the labyrinth of BI has revealed deeper and deeper reflections. Each chapter has shown us how human choices about what to measure, how to measure it, and how to present the results inevitably shape the stories we tell with data. Yet this research, important as it is, has largely focused on the external tools and processes of analysis. Only now, in Chapter 8, do we turn our attention to the most fundamental influence on every number we generate and every conclusion we draw: the cognitive biases that reside in our own minds.

Why devote an entire chapter to cognitive bias at this stage? After all, we've already touched on aspects of psychology in previous discussions of framing effects and the social pressures that accompany polished control panels. But those forays treated bias largely as an unfortunate side effect, an extra wrinkle to be ironed out with better footnotes or more cautious design choices.

To underline this point, consider the progression of our chapters so far. We started by showing how numbers can seduce us with their apparent certainty, then how the wrong inputs can distort those numbers, and finally how misleading patterns can lead us to false causality. We've shown that dashboards, for all their usefulness, can be turned into weapons by design, that averages can hide more than they reveal, and that metrics themselves can be distorted to suit convenient narratives.

In each case, the solution we proposed involved better processes: validation checks, distribution-based reporting, immutable definitions, multi-metric scorecards, etc. These improvements are important, but they all assume that when the data is "clean" and the dashboards are "honest", we will automatically draw accurate conclusions.

This chapter challenges that assumption. It argues that no matter how perfect our systems are, human cognition will continue to look for shortcuts and favor narratives that reinforce existing beliefs. Unless we learn to recognize and counteract these mental shortcuts, we will continue to lead ourselves into analytical dead ends, organizational blind spots, and, sometimes, complete disasters.

INTERPRETATION BIAS: A HUMAN DEFECT

Bias in data analysis is not a rare flaw; it is *our default setting*. Whenever we sit down to explore a spreadsheet or look at a graph, our brains use a series of heuristics designed to simplify a complex world.

Remember how we need less than 5 milliseconds to judge a design or even a person? These shortcuts—anchoring ourselves in initial values, looking for patterns in randomness, and favoring information that confirms what we already think—were powerful survival tools in our ancestral environment. Detecting a rustle in the bushes as a potential predator, for example, was safer than ignoring it and risking disaster. Our minds have evolved to make quick decisions with incomplete data.

In the business world, however, we don't face saber-toothed tigers, but rather the illusion of clarity and rationality. With only a moment to formulate a recommendation or justify a prediction, we unconsciously fill in the gaps with narratives that promise immediacy and coherence. The result is that even the most elaborate algorithms and the most defensible processes end up passing through the sieve of our cognitive biases before informing decisions.

This process often begins with what psychologists call the need for *cognitive closure*—our aversion to uncertainty and ambiguity (Cunff, 2022). Faced with incomplete or contradictory data, the mind feels a subtle discomfort, a tension that demands resolution. To relieve this tension, we readily accept the first plausible explanation we find, even if it is based on shaky foundations.

A constantly rising graph can catch our eye and seem to speak for itself, leading us to draw a confident conclusion: "Our new feature is driving user growth." In the absence of a more in-depth analysis of seasonal effects, cohort analysis, or external confounding factors, we may feel a fleeting sense of relief that we have spotted the trend. Only later, perhaps when the following month's results disappoint us, do we realize that our initial interpretation was premature.

EXPERIENCE AND INGRAINED PATTERNS

Experience and expertise, ironically, can make the bias even stronger. Over time, analysts develop a mental repertoire of familiar patterns, seasonal sales cycles, typical user acquisition curves, and standard cost structures. When new data arrives, the mind instinctively associates it with familiar patterns. If the pattern resembles last quarter's jump due to a price promotion, we conclude that it's the same dynamic, rather than considering new factors such as the launch of a competitor or a change in customer preferences.

This tendency to see what we expect to see is often so automatic that it escapes consciousness. Specialized knowledge becomes a lens that both sharpens and limits perception: it helps us process information quickly, but can blind us to anomalies that don't fit our expectations.

Moreover, the *Dunning-Kruger effect* often exacerbates this situation: less experienced analysts may overestimate the accuracy of their pattern matching, while experienced experts, aware of how little they really know, may doubt valid signals (Mazor & Fleming, 2021). In both cases, poorly calibrated self-assessment leads us to cling to familiar tools and models even when they no longer apply.

Consider the data scientist who has spent years perfecting a regression model to predict demand. That model becomes a trusted tool, its parameters refined to capture subtle regularities in historical data. When the next set of data arrives, for example, demand in a new geographical region, there is a natural impulse to apply the same model, perhaps with minor adjustments, instead of wondering if the relationships might be different. After all, the existing model has served well in the past.

However, if these regional markets have different consumer behaviors, regulatory environments, or competitive scenarios, forcing them to follow yesterday's model will produce misleading forecasts. The trust we place in our tried-and-tested tools thus becomes a liability, a form of overconfidence that blinds us to contextual changes.

THE DANGERS OF DISSONANCE

Closely related to expertise is our desire for internal coherence. We hate discordant notes, data points, or narratives that don't fit perfectly into the story we've constructed. When faced with contradictory signals, we instinctively seek harmony by flattening or excluding discord.

A metric that contradicts a high-level strategic narrative—"Yes, we said that customer satisfaction was increasing, but why is our churn rate going up?"—can seem like an attack on the story itself. To protect ourselves from this discomfort, we may devalue the inconvenient metric as if it were an exception, attribute it to a measurement error, or bury it in a footnote. This impulse to resolve cognitive dissonance is powerful; it leads us to edit the evidence instead of revising our beliefs.

This behavior is not simply evasive; it has real organizational consequences. When teams ignore early warning signs in favor of preserving a coherent narrative, they lose valuable time to adapt strategies. A slight increase in returns may presage a product defect, but the pressure to maintain a constant improvement story can delay root cause analysis. Over time, small unresolved problems accumulate until they become major crises. And by then, it's too late to claim innocence based on the data; the habit of suppressing dissenting information has become an integral part of the analytical culture itself.

Neuroscience has begun to clarify why dissonance is so viscerally uncomfortable: fMRI studies reveal that when people encounter evidence that contradicts their beliefs, the anterior cingulate cortex lights up with signals similar to physical pain or social rejection (van Veen et al., 2009). This "pain of contradiction" leads us to seek mental relief by disregarding or reinterpreting the incompatibility. In practice, this means that each set of slides, spreadsheet pivot, or dashboard filter carries not only information but also emotional weight.

In other words, conflicting data literally "hurts", triggering a fight-or-flight response that diverts our attention to the comforting, consonant evidence. These brain-based findings explain why simply presenting contradictory metrics is not enough; without deliberate interventions, people will almost reflexively disregard any data that threatens their internal narrative.

COMMON COGNITIVE BIASES IN DATA ANALYSIS

Although an exhaustive taxonomy of all mental shortcuts would fill a thesis, there are several biases that stand out for their enormous impact on working with data.

Confirmation bias, perhaps the most notorious, leads us to look for, interpret, and remember information that aligns with our preconceptions. In practice, this resembles hypothesis testing without any real curiosity, running several regressions until one of them produces the p-value we want, or drawing up queries whose parameters assume our preferred outcome. As soon as a preliminary conclusion takes shape, we unconsciously discard or reduce the emphasis on evidence that contradicts it, while giving more importance to supporting observations.

The *anchoring bias* exerts its influence even earlier in the process. The first piece of information we come across—a historical reference, an off-the-cuff observation by a stakeholder, or an initial rough estimate—anchors subsequent judgments. Even when new data suggests a different conclusion, we find it difficult to recalibrate completely. For example, if the initial forecast points to 10,000 new users and our refined analysis points to 7,000, we may continue to report "8,500" in recognition of our anchor, rather than acknowledging the total downward revision.

The *availability bias* leads us to overvalue information that is vivid, recent, or emotionally charged. A complaint from a high-profile customer or a sensationalist story in the media can seem more important than a sea of routine feedback. We can then allocate disproportionate resources to investigating and resolving the anecdote, neglecting more systemic but less dramatic issues. This tendency is exacerbated in dashboards that highlight outliers in bright red or cheer fluctuations, leading stakeholders to fixate on sensational deviations rather than overall trends.

Overconfidence bias, common among experienced analysts, adds another layer of risk. Experience breeds confidence, and confidence often breeds the assumption that one's models, interpretations, and recommendations are more accurate than they actually are. Overconfidence can lead to insufficient testing of alternative models, muted cautionary language in reports, and a reluctance to ask for critical feedback. Analysts learn to trust their intuition and past successes, even when data contexts change and new uncertainties arise.

Framing effects are also felt at all stages of analysis. The same data can be presented in ways that evoke totally different impressions: absolute dollar changes versus percentage changes, month-on-month comparisons versus year-on-year comparisons, cumulative totals versus period-on-period figures. Two reports, each technically correct, can send diametrically opposed messages simply through the choice of baseline or the decision to normalize by a certain denominator. Small framing choices thus become powerful levers for shaping stakeholder perceptions.

The *optimism bias and the planning fallacy* together lead to overly optimistic projections. We constantly overestimate our ability to execute projects on time and within budget, assuming best-case scenarios and discounting common delays, integration obstacles, and resource constraints. Implementing a data platform scheduled for six months often takes a year, and an algorithm expected to increase conversions by 20 percent may take five. However, both analysts and stakeholders tend to attribute these failures to unpredictable "external factors," rather than recognizing the systematic optimism of our forecasts.

The *survivor bias* leads us to analyze only the successes that have lasted, neglecting the many failed experiments and abandoned initiatives that could teach us fundamental lessons. When we celebrate the handful of models that proved to be robust, we risk ignoring the dozens that fell apart when faced with new data or new business conditions. This creates the illusion that good results are more reliable and repeatable than they really are.

Retrospective bias makes the challenge even worse. Once an outcome is known, our memories and testimonies are reframed to suggest that "we knew it all along". This fallacy of inevitability prevents genuine learning because we underestimate the role of chance and ambiguity in past decisions. Teams leave autopsies believing they had a foresight that they didn't really have, and so they don't reinforce the processes that could have detected or mitigated errors in real time.

GROUP DYNAMICS: ECHO CHAMBERS AND GROUPTHINK

The individual prejudices described above are multiplied when the analysis is carried out in a group. Organizations often form teams of like-minded individuals: data scientists with similar backgrounds, product managers with parallel career paths, or executives who share a common worldview.

In these *echo chambers*, the dominant narrative reverberates unchallenged, reinforcing assumptions and marginalizing disagreements. Alternative points of view, which may highlight overlooked variables or propose unconventional interpretations, are quickly drowned out.

Groupthink arises when the desire for harmony or conformity leads the group to reach a consensus without critically evaluating alternative ideas. In a close-knit team, raising uncomfortable issues can feel like a social betrayal. Junior analysts learn that disagreement invites social friction or damage to their reputation. As a result, the team unites around a single story, often the one presented by the most senior or vocal member, while the underlying uncertainties and disagreements remain unresolved.

Illusions of consensus further distort decision-making. A unanimous vote on a proposed strategy or model can seem like a validation of its correctness: "If everyone agrees, it must be right". However, unanimity often reflects social pressure rather than independent analysis. When stakeholders see collective buy-in, they become more confident in the group's conclusions and less likely to review the data or question the underlying assumptions. This momentum pushes recommendations forward without sufficient barriers, leaving little room for course correction when new data emerges.

CULTIVATING COGNITIVE AWARENESS: DEFENSIVE STRATEGIES

Confronting this constellation of prejudices and group dynamics requires deliberate countermeasures, both procedural and cultural.

Firstly, organizations should institutionalize moments of *"slow reflection"*, during which teams pause to question assumptions, explore alternative explanations, and rehearse counterarguments. Techniques such as the *pre-mortem*: imagining that a project has failed catastrophically and brainstorming the reasons why—make it possible to consider the confounding factors before they arise. *Devil's advocate roles*, whether rotating or formally assigned, encourage teams to subject prevailing hypotheses to rigorous critique without social penalty.

Secondly, processes should require *explicit documentation of assumptions*, anchors, and framing choices at each stage of the analysis. When building a model or designing a control panel, the initial choices—why we started the time series in January, why we excluded certain segments, why we prioritized absolute counts over percentages—should be recorded along with the results. This record of provenance makes it difficult to hide changes in the framework and makes it easier to review initial decisions if new data calls them into question.

Thirdly, cross-functional analysis and the *rotation of team members* help put an end to echo chambers. By inviting stakeholders from different backgrounds—customer support, finance, operations, marketing—to examine reviews at key moments, organizations ensure that diverse perspectives investigate assumptions and highlight blind spots. These reviews need not unduly delay execution; even brief, structured check-ins can bring out critical questions that would otherwise not be asked.

Finally, ongoing *training in cognitive bias and decision science* can increase collective awareness. Workshops, case studies, and facilitated discussions on real catastrophes, where uncontrolled bias led to disastrous outcomes, make abstract concepts more evident. Learning becomes relevant rather than theoretical by linking bias training directly to organizational priorities and historical examples from the company.

FINAL THOUGHTS

Cognitive biases permeate every corner of our lives, shaping the way we perceive the world, form our beliefs, and consolidate our values. From the choices we make in the supermarket to the causes we champion on social media, our minds rely on shortcuts that seem easy but can lead us astray.

In the field of BI and data analysis, these same shortcuts subtly distort our interpretations, leading us to what is familiar, comfortable, and convenient. Recognizing this is not a concession of defeat; on the contrary, it is an invitation to bring all our humanity to the analytical process, to turn the very biases that blind us into signals for deeper investigation.

This chapter has shown that even the cleanest data, the most transparent models, and the most honest dashboards cannot protect us from the mental filters through which we view them. However, therein lies an opportunity. Data analysis becomes not only a vehicle for external insights, but a mirror for our own internal narratives. Every time we catch ourselves dismissing a discrepancy or overvaluing a trend that confirms our hunches, we gain a moment to pause, question our assumptions, and perhaps recalibrate our analysis and our wider worldview.

We've discussed many biases, such as confirmation bias, anchoring, overconfidence, and the pain of cognitive dissonance, and it's important to remember that these are just a sample of the mental shortcuts at play. Others, like the *Bandwagon Effect*, lead us to align our conclusions with the opinion of the majority simply because it's popular, while the status quo bias keeps us stuck with outdated metrics and practices long after they've outlived their usefulness.

Countless lesser-known heuristics lurk beneath the surface, each capable of distorting decisions in subtle but impactful ways. The key is to develop the habit of doing mental *"bias audits"*, continually asking: "Which of my own thought patterns might be influencing this interpretation?"

To complicate matters further, analysts and stakeholders rarely share identical mental models. We often *fail to explain* the nuances of our analysis, assuming a shared framework that doesn't exist. In the resulting void, other people naturally fill in the gaps with their own predispositions, be they optimism, skepticism, or simply the recurrence of a vivid anecdote. To avoid this, clear communication must accompany each number: explain not only what, but also how and why. Structured guidelines, annotated dashboards, and explicit discussions of uncertainties help to align mental models and keep everyone on track.

Group dynamics also amplify these challenges. In addition to the echo chambers and groupthink we've already examined, *group polarization* can push consensus views to extremes, as like-minded teams reinforce each other's prejudices until they become unrecognizable. What started out as a cautious assumption turns into near certainty, and dissenting voices, especially the more cautious or contrarian perspectives, are quietly pushed aside. To combat this, deliberate processes are needed: rotating team members, inviting external reviewers, and scheduling "pre-mortems", where imagining failure becomes a constructive exercise rather than an uncomfortable anomaly.

At its best, data analysis is a disciplined practice of intellectual humility, a constant interplay between curiosity and skepticism. When we recognize the psychological pressures that shape every pivot table, chart, and forecast, we equip ourselves to ask better questions, design more robust protections, and create a culture in which admitting uncertainty is not seen as a failure, but as an asset.

In the next chapter, we'll leave the laboratory of our minds and enter the realm of principles and responsibility, showing the *ethical dilemmas* that lie at the heart of every decision.

We'll see how the choices we make about defining, collecting, and using data can improve or harm real people. These discussions will give us a moral compass for BI, reminding us that technical rigor alone is not enough; we must also ask ourselves what we should be doing.

CHAPTER 9

THE ETHICS OF DATA MANIPULATION

> *Errors using inadequate data are much less than those using no data at all.*
>
> — CHARLES BABBAGE

Every time we cut up a data set, choose one metric over another, decide which story to tell or which nuance to hide, we make a moral choice.

In the previous chapters, we cataloged the many techniques by which metrics can be bent, reframed, or completely distorted to serve certain ends. We learned how a simple change in a denominator, the selective cutting of a time window, or the framing of a statistic in absolute or percentage terms can transform the apparent meaning of the most sober-looking numbers.

But knowledge of these techniques alone does not tell us when their use is defensible and when it crosses the line into ethical misconduct. This chapter addresses that question.

We explore the boundary between legitimate data refinement and deceptive manipulation, examine the motives behind these choices, and consider the very real human and institutional costs of letting expediency prevail over sincerity.

If the previous chapters showed us how to cheat with numbers, this chapter asks: Is it always right to do so?

WHEN DOES DATA MANIPULATION CROSS THE LINE?

Data analysis is an art of *refinement*. We have to impute missing values, resolve schema inconsistencies, align definitions between systems, and abstract complex results into digestible knowledge. Each of these steps involves decisions, such as how to deal with atypical values, whether to aggregate or disaggregate, and which visual encodings best convey nuances.

Ethical professionals embrace *transparency*: they document their cleaning rules, note changes in settings, and accompany each dashboard with warnings about coverage, sampling error, and version history. These practices recognize that the path from raw data to final metrics is fraught with interpretive bifurcations and that clarity about these choices strengthens, rather than weakens, trust.

In contrast, deceptive manipulation chooses metrics and frames the results with the primary aim of *misleading*. The same act of omitting data from a particular region, smoothing out erratic peaks, or reframing growth based on a conveniently low baseline becomes unethical when the motive is to conceal inconvenient truths rather than to improve methodological rigor.

A pharmaceutical company that excludes data on adverse reactions from a safety report because they don't fit the regulatory definitions is crossing the line; a medical researcher who omits such data because the sample size is statistically too small to draw reliable conclusions is acting responsibly, as long as the omission is fully disclosed.

Intention, therefore, lies at the heart of the ethical divide. If our aim is to illuminate reality to give stakeholders a more accurate basis for judgment, then framing choices that highlight certain angles may be defensible. If our aim is to persuade decision-makers to come to a predetermined conclusion, to gloss over risks, or to create a veneer of steady progress, then we are betraying the trust that data grants us.

Even the medium doesn't excuse manipulation. A pie chart that omits a problematic slice is as dishonest as an Excel sheet that hides a column, and perhaps more insidious precisely because it looks so polished.

Different sectors face different ethical risks. In corporate finance, the pressure to meet quarterly targets can lead to aggressive revenue recognition or the reclassification of operating expenses as one-off charges. Practices that, while sometimes falling within the gray areas of accounting standards, erode long-term credibility when exposed.

In politics, the selective presentation of crime or unemployment figures can influence public opinion and distort democratic processes. In marketing, agencies learn early on that "embellishing" campaign metrics is rewarded with bigger budgets and renewed contracts, leaving consumers and clients with an inflated sense of effectiveness. In public policy, research organizations can discreetly hide negative study results to safeguard funding, thus depriving legislators of a balanced evidence base.

In each of these areas, the temptation to distort data for immediate gain is matched only by the seriousness of the possible consequences when the true figures come to light.

THE SLIPPERY SLOPE OF JUSTIFYING DATA MANIPULATION

Analysts rarely set out to commit major fraud. More often, they commit gradual slips, rationalizing each choice as a harmless or even necessary adjustment. "Let's just smooth out this peak, it's clearly an anomaly". "Let's compare it to our lowest performing region to show the potential for growth." "I'll convert these absolute figures into percentages; it's easier for the public to digest." Each concession may seem trivial in isolation, but together they accumulate into a mosaic of distortion.

This can be called *moral licensing*: when we give ourselves permission for a small ethical violation, we become more willing to commit larger ones. A junior analyst who omits a few anomalous data points because they "distort the story" can then justify hiding a whole subset of underperforming sales records. Soon, the cumulative effect is that half the data ends up off the table, and the narrative is crafted, step by step, to present only a rosy picture.

The fallacy that *the end justifies the means* further erodes ethical protections. If leadership believes that presenting favorable statistics will ensure buy-in for a critical innovation that will ultimately benefit customers or society, it can tacitly tolerate the "creative" presentation of data.

Indeed, teams often hear refrains such as "We need the board to fund this, so use the numbers to our advantage". But even noble objectives cannot sanctify a dishonest presentation; when the smoke clears, stakeholders learn not only the true situation but also the deception that covered it up. The longer the subterfuge, the bigger the balance sheet, and the more costly the loss of credibility.

Organizations also play a role in promoting or resisting this drift. A culture that rewards the most optimistic metrics above all else implicitly indicates that the ends take precedence over integrity. On the other hand, organizations that value candor, even when the numbers aren't flattering, encourage analysts to reveal problems at an early stage, to treat confusing truths as opportunities for course correction, and to view transparency as a strategic asset rather than a tactical inconvenience.

ETHICAL GRAY AREAS IN DATA COMMUNICATION

Not all ethical dilemmas are black and white. Many arise in a murky terrain where it is difficult to discern the difference between simplification and distortion. A communications executive can justifiably condense a complex 20-page report into a single infographic. However, in doing so, he has to decide which of the dozens of nuances to omit.

At what point does simplification for the sake of clarity become misrepresentation by omission?

- **Simplification vs. distortion:** Busy executives crave succinct headlines: "Sales increased by 12%" instead of a 15-page report on demographic changes, seasonality, and currency fluctuations. But oversimplification can hide critical warnings. A public health panel that reports that "95% of patients responded positively" without clarifying the severity of the side effects risks misleading both doctors and patients, even if no data was intentionally withheld. Distortion begins when simplification removes the essential context for understanding. The ethical question is: does the simplified message still, on balance, convey a fair picture?
- **Framing the data for persuasion:** We choose whether to emphasize absolute counts or percentage changes, whether to anchor growth figures in annual bases or monthly fluctuations, and whether to plot time series with zero-based or truncated axes. Persuasive framing is an intrinsic part of data storytelling; good communicators know how to use visual emphasis to draw attention to important trends. However, when framing choices systematically hide declines, amplify small rises, or exploit cognitive biases (such as using red to signal neutral changes), they cross over into manipulation.
- **Conscious use of incomplete data:** Any analysis is based on incomplete data; some variables are not observed, and some populations are not represented. Ethical data practice requires

acknowledging these shortcomings: "We couldn't record the turnover of 20% of our clients because they bypassed our login system." Failing to point out these omissions creates a false sense of completeness. Worse still, the deliberate omission of inconvenient segments, knowing that these segments would weaken a marketing argument or management presentation, constitutes unethical manipulation.

- **Algorithmic black boxes:** As organizations increasingly rely on machine learning and automated decision systems, they are confronted with ethical gray areas around model opacity. A supplier can provide a "proprietary" credit scoring algorithm without revealing how it weights demographic factors. If the model systematically disadvantages certain groups, but users never discover the bias because the code is hidden, is that manipulation? While intellectual property concerns may justify some secrecy, the ethical imperative remains: decisions that materially affect people's lives, such as credit approvals, job selection, and insurance underwriting require transparency, auditability, and recourse.

In each of these areas, the boundary between improvement and deception depends on intention, audience expectations, and the degree of transparency. When audiences are aware of simplifications, framing choices, or model assumptions, and when they have the means to investigate further, then ethical risks decrease. However, when these choices are hidden, audiences are led to assume that they are complete and neutral, and any selective modeling becomes a betrayal of trust.

THE CONSEQUENCES OF UNETHICAL DATA PRACTICES

The risks of misleading data go far beyond annoyances or bruised egos. Organizations that trade short-term reputational gains for long-term trust often find that the losses outweigh any immediate benefits.

When misleading statistics are exposed, whether by investigative journalists, whistleblowers, or independent auditors, the public reaction can be swift and relentless, consumers and citizens, feeling betrayed, withdraw their trust. Investors sell shares. Political opponents take advantage of the scandal. Rebuilding credibility can take years, if it ever happens.

Legal and financial repercussions often follow. In the business sphere, regulators have imposed heavy fines on banks and companies that misled investors with falsified performance indicators. Class action and shareholder lawsuits can inflict billions of dollars in damages. In the health sector, pharmaceutical companies that have manipulated clinical trial data face crushing penalties, as well as the loss of public and professional trust that no fine can fully repair.

In addition to institutions, *people* suffer serious damage when data is used incorrectly. Credit rating agencies that hide the true composition of their risk models can wrongly deny loans to qualified borrowers. Healthcare providers who exaggerate the effectiveness of treatments can expose patients to undue risk. When selecting job candidates, black box algorithms can filter out multiple candidates based on correlations that have no causal relationship to job performance, reinforcing systemic prejudices and fueling social inequality.

The issue is existential: *manipulated data can determine whether someone gets a house, obtains life-saving medication, or has access to opportunities.*

In public policy, the selective presentation of statistical trends distorts civic debate. Municipalities that don't record crime or exaggerate school completion rates create false impressions of progress and can deter necessary reforms. Advocacy groups that emphasize one statistic and omit contrary data can polarize discourse and erode faith in the neutrality of fact-finding. As data becomes the new terrain of political contestation, the integrity of numbers is fundamental to a healthy democracy.

When prominent cases of data fraud come to light, the knock-on effects extend to entire sectors. Regulators respond with stricter disclosure requirements; data platforms impose stricter governance controls; customers demand third-party audits. While these measures may strengthen overall accountability, they also increase compliance burdens and slow down innovation. In the rush to police bad actors, well-intentioned professionals can find themselves caught in a rising tide of suspicion.

ASSESSING THE ETHICS OF USING DATA

Evaluating ethics requires more than intuition intended for this purpose; it requires deliberate structures and disciplined analysis.

- **Ask probing questions:** Before sharing any analysis, ask yourself and your team these three questions:
  - Would I trust this data if I were receiving it? Role reversal helps reveal subconscious rationalizations.
  - Am I presenting the whole truth or just a selective version? Question all omissions: what has been left out of the set of slides, and why?
  - Would this hold up under public and legal scrutiny? Imagine journalists, regulators, or competitors dissecting your work. If you feel exposed, you need to be more transparent.
- **Ethical review advice:** Data projects, especially those with a significant social impact, such as clinical trials, algorithmic contracting tools, or public policy analysis, should be subject to formal ethical review. These interdisciplinary panels, drawing on legal, technical, and domain expertise, assess assumptions, sampling methods, framing choices, and disclosure practices. When disagreements arise, the board may require additional sensitivity analyses or demand that uncertainties be disclosed more visibly.
- **Documentation and audit trails:** Each transformation, whether filtering, imputation, or redefinition, must be recorded in an accessible repository. Version control is not just a

development best practice; it's an ethical imperative. When a dashboard changes its KPI definitions, the previous versions, the justification for the change, and the announcement to stakeholders should be publicly recorded. This transparency discourages covert manipulation and provides a clear path for audit and post-mortem analysis.

- **Ethics training and certification:** Just as doctors and lawyers adhere to codes of conduct, data professionals benefit from formal training in ethics. Case studies, from Enron's accounting tricks to Cambridge Analytica's misuse of social media profiles, underpin abstract principles with real consequences. Certification programs can help embed a shared vocabulary of data ethics, ensuring that teams recognize not only technical errors but also moral failings.
- **Stakeholder involvement:** Whenever possible, involve affected communities in the design and interpretation of data projects. Community advisory panels, customer focus groups, or public comment periods reveal concerns about representation, framing, and potential harm. Involving stakeholders at an early stage democratizes the process and eliminates ethical blind spots that insiders may overlook.
- **Safe channels for whistleblowing:** Professionals must have confidential channels to raise ethical concerns without fear of reprisals. Whether through ombudsman offices, anonymous hotlines, or secure email systems, these channels must

guarantee serious follow-up. Organizations that suppress or ignore whistleblowing invite systemic decay.

Ethical data practice is not a one-off launch, but a continuous path.. Regular workshops, seminars, and guest speakers help teams keep an eye on emerging challenges such as privacy regulations, advances in AI explainability, or new ways of manipulating metrics. Cultures that institutionalize reflection and debate are more resistant to complacency and drift.

FUNDAMENTAL PRINCIPLES OF ETHICAL DATA MANAGEMENT

Based on these evaluation mechanisms and the General Data Protection Regulation (GDPR) protection principles (Wolford, 2024), we can articulate five fundamental principles that should guide every organization's relationship with data. Together, they form a compass for responsible decision-making.

Respect for Ownership and Consent

- **Definition:** Individuals retain control over any data that can identify or reflect their behavior.
- **Practice:** Collect only with explicit and informed consent, whether through clear privacy policies, opt-in dialogues, or signed agreements. Never assume tacit approval; each data point must go back to a deliberate choice by the user. Accept requests to delete or restrict data promptly and without charge.

Radical Transparency

- **Definition:** Data collection methods, processing algorithms, and analytical assumptions should be openly disclosed.
- **Practice:** Publish documentation that explains what data you collect, how you store it, what transformations you apply, and why. On dashboards, accompany each metric with tooltips or footnotes detailing its genesis and any recently applied changes. When the audience sees exactly how the numbers were obtained, they can interpret the results with the proper context and challenge them when necessary.

Vigilant Privacy and Security

- **Definition:** Protecting personal information from unauthorized exposure is an ethical imperative.
- **Practice:** Implement strong technical safeguards such as encryption at rest, two-factor authentication, strict access controls, and organizational policies such as regular security audits. Where full identifiers are unnecessary, anonymize or pseudonymize data sets to minimize the risk of re-identification. Treat privacy as an ongoing commitment and not a one-off checkbox.

Purpose-Driven Data Minimization

- **Definition:** Collect only the data that is essential to meet legitimate, predefined objectives.

- **Practice:** Before adding fields to a database or asking new survey questions, ask: "How will this data inform decisions and improve results?" If a data element does not directly serve a defined purpose, exclude it. This principle reduces mission drift, limits exposure, and ensures that analysis remains firmly aligned with real-world value and not idle curiosities.

Responsibility for Results and Equity

- **Definition:** Ethical analysis requires anticipating and taking responsibility for the social impact of a project.
- **Practice:** Conduct thorough impact assessments examining not only average effects, but also potential disparate impacts on vulnerable groups. Create feedback loops to monitor real-world consequences and be prepared to modify or remove algorithms that produce unfair or harmful results. When harm occurs, acknowledge it openly, correct it, and share lessons learned to prevent it from happening again.

FINAL THOUGHTS

The tension between clarity and frankness, between persuasion and truth, is inherent in any endeavor that transforms complex realities into digestible numbers. All data professionals, from the novice analyst to the top executive, carry the burden of managing this transformation responsibly. Technical proficiency, while necessary, is not enough; ethical discernment must guide all choices, from the first line of data cleansing code to the final executive summary.

Creating a transparent organizational culture that regularly discloses limitations, sources, and uncertainties; that documents the definitions and evolution of metrics; and that promotes secure reporting of irregularities is a moral imperative and a strategic advantage. At a time when public trust in institutions is fragile, honesty becomes an asset: stakeholders reward candor with loyalty, regulators relieve excessive scrutiny, and employees take pride in their integrity.

However, ethics cannot be based on individual virtue alone. It requires robust processes such as ethical review boards, audit trails, safe whistleblowing mechanisms, and leaders willing to elevate difficult truths above short-term optics. When data manipulation moves from legitimate refinement to deception, the consequences transcend balance sheets and dashboards; they strike at the very foundations of informed decision-making and social cohesion.

In the next chapter, we will move from questions of intent and ethics to *concrete examples of data disasters*. We will examine real-world case studies: from volatile financial forecasts that triggered market crashes, to health crises exacerbated by hidden uncertainties, to civic initiatives undermined by skewed public opinion metrics, and trace how the interplay of manipulated numbers, cognitive biases, and organizational pressures converged to produce human and institutional harm.

CHAPTER 10

REAL-WORLD DISASTERS

> It's easy to lie with statistics. It's hard to tell the truth without statistics.
>
> — ANDREJS DUNKELS

When the term "data-driven" became the watchword of modern management, many believed that rigorous analysis would finally banish guesswork, inoculate decisions against bias, and deliver superior results in finance, business, government, and medicine. In boardrooms and briefing rooms alike, executives envisioned dashboards filled with real-time metrics, algorithms poised to reveal hidden patterns, and statistical models that offered accurate predictions.

Data, it seemed, would become a kind of secular oracle, guiding resource allocation, product roadmaps, public policy, and patient care with an unbiased hand. However, as history has repeatedly shown, numbers alone are no remedy for human fallibility. On the contrary, misplaced faith in flawed data, or worse, the deliberate manipulation of metrics, has precipitated some of the most devastating economic collapses, business collapses, political failures, and public health tragedies of the last half-century.

In this chapter, we walk through cautionary tales spanning global finance, Silicon Valley startups, ancient corporate titans, centralized and democratic governments, academic labs, healthcare institutions, aerospace engineering, and more to reveal an unsettling truth: data is not a panacea. Without skepticism, domain expertise, and robust ethical protections, our most sophisticated models can become elaborate smokescreens, our most cherished metrics seductive illusions, and our most reliable algorithms vehicles of mass delusion.

As we examine each of the stories, four themes will resonate: the danger of confusing mathematical sophistication with infallibility; the corrosive power of Goodhart's Law, which warns that when a measure becomes a target, it is no longer a reliable indicator; the weight of cultural and cognitive biases that silence dissent and amplify blind spots; and the human temptation to distort, select or obfuscate numbers for short-term gain. We will further understand that building a truly resilient data culture requires not only technical fixes but also organizational humility, transparent governance, continuous audit trails, and a willingness to empower skeptics and believers alike.

FINANCIAL CRISES: HOW BAD DATA DESTROYED ECONOMIES

Few episodes in modern history sum up the dangers of misplaced faith in complex models better than the collapse of the subprime *mortgage market in 2008*.

During the early 2000s, Wall Street operated under the triumphant belief that statistical analysis and financial engineering had finally tamed risk. Banks and rating agencies used the *Gaussian copula*, a mathematical formula designed to model the probability of several loans defaulting simultaneously. By assuming that real estate market declines in different regions of the U.S. were effectively independent, the copula generated extremely small estimates of the risk of joint default. If mortgages in Florida, California, and Ohio were not correlated, the logic was that issuing bonds that pooled thousands of individual home loans could yield almost risk-free returns: diversification had beaten chance (Salmon, 2009).

The elegance of the copula and the triple-A ratings given to collateralized debt obligations (CDOs) created from its results led investors to create ever more elaborate structures. Synthetic CDOs, layered derivatives, and "risk transfers" became the hallmarks of quantitative prowess.

But beneath the veneer of sophisticated code lay two fatal flaws. First, the assumption of independence collapsed when housing prices across the country fell in tandem, fueled by rising interest rates, rampant loan fraud, and a crumbling national credit bubble.

Secondly, the rating agencies, paid by the very issuers whose CDOs they rated, faced an inherent conflict of interest. Eager to earn lucrative fees, they applied the copula generously, assigning the highest grades to products that, unbeknownst to the buyers, rested on the shaky ground of adjustable-rate mortgages issued to borrowers with weak documentation.

When defaults increased, the statistical walls crumbled. Banks found themselves in possession of apparently diversified portfolios that suddenly behaved as if each mortgage had identical exposure. Liquidity froze, balance sheets imploded, and, in September 2008, the venerable investment bank Lehman Brothers collapsed, triggering a cascade of government bailouts and a global recession that wiped out trillions in household wealth.

The 2008 crisis was not the first time the financial markets had been damaged by the dangers of bad data, nor would it be the last.

In the late 1990s, during the *dot-com* boom, investors and venture capitalists awarded billions based on vanity metrics such as "page views", "unique visitors," and "eyeballs". Webvan, an ambitious mail-order grocery start-up, raised more than 800 million dollars, promising to scale same-day delivery nationwide. Its founder praised user registration counts and website traffic as proof of insatiable demand while ignoring the consumption rate needed to stock warehouses, maintain truck fleets, and fulfill low-margin orders (Barr, 2013). Pets.com, another of the darling companies of the time, splurged on national TV ads (with a catchy sock mascot) while ignoring the unit economics of shipping heavy pet products.

When the funding taps ran dry, both companies collapsed spectacularly, leaving behind empty storefronts in the virtual market and fortunes lost to early backers. The dot-com bust offered a very clear lesson: *raw engagement metrics, disconnected from genuine willingness to pay, can masquerade as signs of sustainable business models.*

BUSINESS FAILURES: WHEN COMPANIES BET ON THE WRONG DATA

The dangers of relying too much on superficial metrics go far beyond emerging Internet companies. In 2000, *Blockbuster* Video, at the time the undisputed king of home entertainment rentals, had the opportunity to acquire *Netflix* for 50 million dollars (Chong, 2015). Blockbuster's management, armed with detailed data on franchise foot traffic, revenues from late fees, and the number of customers in stores, rejected the offer. Their metrics showed a picture of continued strength for physical store rentals, and they dismissed Hastings' DVD-by-mail subscription model as a niche curiosity.

Meanwhile, Netflix quietly scaled up its logistics, perfected its recommendation algorithm, and built a subscriber base at a modest cost. Blockbuster, distracted by store-level metrics and cash flows from late fees, failed to detect the growing discontent among customers who hated expiration dates and valued unlimited rentals. Within a decade, Blockbuster filed for bankruptcy; Netflix, freed from the long-overdue takeover debate, ushered in the era of subscription streaming.

Most recently, the failed experiment known as *Quibi* highlights how completion rates and time watched statistics can lull investors into a false sense of traction.

Launched in April 2020 with nearly $2 billion in funding, Quibi marketed itself as "quick bites" of Hollywood-level content optimized for mobile consumption. Executives cited high completion rates, above 80% for many episodes, as a proof that viewers found the format appealing. However, completion rates only measure whether someone who pressed "play" stayed to the end of a ten-minute video; they don't tell us anything about whether viewers became paid subscribers, whether they returned after the free trial, or whether they recommended the platform to friends. When Quibi's free trial ended, cancellations far outnumbered new sign-ups. Within eight months, the company closed its doors, a reminder that engagement metrics separated from user retention and revenue streams can be dangerously misleading (Statt, 2020).

The story of the *Ford Edsel* is a mid-century cautionary tale about over-legislated market research.

In 1957, Ford invested 250 million dollars in developing a new model that it hoped would bridge the gap between its blue-collar customer base and aspirational buyers. Executives commissioned extensive consumer surveys on every conceivable dimension: from hood ornament design to price tolerance (Time, 1959). But these surveys suffered from aspirational bias: respondents told researchers what they thought sounded sophisticated, not what they would actually buy. Worse still, Ford's sample was heavily geared toward urban and middle-class areas, where buyers were less representative of the broad demographic diversity of the American car market.

When the Edsel was launched, its gaudy styling, various trim levels, and mechanical idiosyncrasies put off both budget-conscious drivers and luxury buyers. First-year sales barely reached 100,000 units, far below the projections of 200,000. Ford eventually wrote off 350 million dollars (more than 3 billion dollars today) and dismantled the Edsel division, which became a symbol of folly geared toward research rather than product innovation.

Perhaps no other scandal better embodies the ethical abyss of manipulated metrics than the rise and fall of *Theranos*. Founded in 2003 by Elizabeth Holmes, a Stanford dropout turned charismatic CEO, Theranos promised to revolutionize blood diagnostics.

Its much-praised "Edison" devices claimed to perform hundreds of tests on a single drop of blood, promising faster and cheaper results than conventional laboratories. Investors eagerly poured in more than 700 million dollars, bringing the company's valuation close to 10 billion dollars. High-level board members and selective trial data lent an aura of credibility (Bilton, 2016).

However, company insiders revealed a darker truth: Edison machines were only used for a small number of analytes; most tests were carried out on third-party instruments, with negative results discarded or altered to suit the desired results. When regulatory agencies and journalists discovered the systematic data selection and misrepresentation,

Theranos collapsed almost overnight. Holmes and other executives faced criminal charges, while Silicon Valley's reputation for hubris-driven innovation suffered a lasting blow.

GOVERNMENT FAILURES: WHEN POLITICAL DECISIONS ARE BASED ON INCORRECT DATA

The temptations of manipulated metrics are not limited to private companies. Governments can also fall victim to incorrect or misleading data that misguides policy, undermines public confidence, and causes widespread damage.

In centrally planned economies, data manipulation was integrated into the very fabric of economic management. In the last decades of the *Soviet Union*, factory and collective farm managers faced strict production quotas dictated by Gosplan, the central planning authority.

To avoid the severe penalties for failing to meet targets, which ranged from demotion to imprisonment, many simply inflated production reports. Steel mills claimed to produce more tons than their furnaces could produce; collective farms boasted of impossible harvests, despite fields left fallow. Relying on these falsified figures, Gosplan allocated raw materials, spare parts, and labor according to a mirage of industrial performance.

Meanwhile, consumer goods became scarce as resources were diverted to the "measured" sectors. The systemic corruption of data contributed directly to economic stagnation, the maldistribution of resources, and, ultimately, the dissolution of the Soviet state itself (Harrison, 2009).

In democracies, overconfidence in forecasting models has also wreaked havoc. Consider *Hurricane Katrina* in August 2005, when faulty hydrological data and outdated levee design parameters left New Orleans catastrophically vulnerable. Engineers based the levee system on historical surge frequencies that underestimated the threat of a category 5 storm. When Katrina hit, the water rose above the design limits, breaching the walls and flooding 80% of the city.

The evacuation plans, drawn up based on outdated population surveys and static flood zone maps, failed to take into account the city's changing demographics and urban sprawl. Federal, state, and local agencies, operating with incompatible data sets and leadership biases, responded too slowly. In the end, more than 1,800 lives were lost, property damage exceeded $100 billion, and FEMA's credibility was shattered (Select Bipartisan Committee, 2006).

The *COVID-19 pandemic*, which emerged in early 2020, revealed the danger of inconsistent epidemiological data and the political risks of manipulating metrics.

In the first weeks of the outbreak, limited testing capacity masked the true scale of infections; the count of confirmed cases reflected both the expansion of capacity and the dynamics of transmission. Jurisdictions implemented disparate definitions for "COVID-related death": some counted only laboratory-confirmed fatalities, while others included 'probable' or 'suspect' cases attributed to the virus.

Deaths in nursing homes often arrive weeks late, distorting real-time mortality curves. Policymakers used these unstable figures to determine the timing and severity of lockdowns, school closures, and hospital capacity expansions. Public confidence waned, as reported infection growth sometimes followed increased testing rather than genuine community spread.

When authorities recalibrated case-counting methodologies (raising or lowering hospitalizations and deaths), they provoked waves of confusion and political backlash. The tragic truth is that standardized and transparent data definitions and real-time auditing systems could have saved lives by enabling more calibrated and timely responses (Khimm et al., 2020).

HEALTH AND SCIENCE: WHEN BAD DATA COSTS LIVES

Nowhere is the human cost of manipulated or flawed data more visceral than in the areas of health and biomedical research. At stake are lives saved or lost, therapies advanced or abandoned, and hope nurtured or betrayed, just as we have seen with COVID-19.

In the late 1990s, *Purdue Pharma* launched OxyContin with marketing materials that proclaimed an "extremely low" risk of addiction. This claim was based on a single short-term clinical study involving fewer than 150 patients, none of whom had a history of substance abuse (Civil action, 2018).

Purdue aggressively funded continuing medical education programs, wrote supportive articles in journals, and encouraged sales representatives to promote OxyContin even for mild chronic pain. Prescription rates soared. In two decades, more than half a million Americans died from opioid overdoses. When internal memos surfaced during the litigation, revealing that Purdue executives knew full well about the risks of addiction, the company faced billions in settlements. However, the cost to public health of thousands of orphaned families and devastated communities cannot be measured in fines.

The *reproducibility crisis* in academic science has also exposed how fabricated or hand-picked data can make entire fields unviable.

In 2014, two articles published in Nature claimed that a brief treatment with acid could convert adult cells into stem cells. Laboratories around the world rushed to reproduce the results, imagining a cheap and accessible path to regenerative medicine. Within a few months, the replication attempts failed; investigations revealed doctored images and impossible experimental records. Nature retracted the articles, the lead researcher resigned in disgrace, and millions in research funding disappeared into a black hole of false promises (Nature, 2014).

Similar scandals have occurred in psychology, where a single influential article on "power poses" inspired corporate workshops and welfare programs before being debunked; in economics, flawed regressions shaped fiscal policies that later fell apart under real-world pressures.

Meanwhile, *artificial intelligence tools*, which have already been heralded as the future of personalized medicine, had problems when confronted with broader populations.

IBM's Watson for Oncology, trained on a restricted group of cancer cases at Memorial Sloan Kettering, excelled in selected demonstrations, recommending treatments in close collaboration with specialist oncologists. However, when deployed in hospitals serving diverse patient populations with different ethnicities, comorbidities, and care protocols, Watson's suggestions occasionally put patients at risk by proposing inapplicable chemotherapy regimens or outdated protocols (Pennestrì et al., 2025).

The system's creators had adjusted too much to the training data and failed to create robust external validation pipelines. Across public sector healthcare systems, algorithmic risk stratification models trained on historical arrest or health claims data reproduced racial and socioeconomic biases, leading to disproportionate monitoring of minority patients and more severe denials of insurance coverage.

These examples underscore a vital lesson: technical sophistication and "big data" platforms are no substitute for rigorous clinical testing, transparent validation, and the oversight of subject matter experts.

OTHER DISASTERS: BEYOND THE OBVIOUS

While finance, corporate strategy, public policy, and medicine have provided the most dramatic stories, data failures extend to all domains where measurement shapes decisions. Aerospace engineering, automotive safety, and high-frequency trading have all witnessed how erroneous or manipulated data can exact a heavy price.

Between October 2018 and March 2019, *two Boeing 737 MAX jets* crashed in Indonesia and Ethiopia, killing 346 people. The culprit was the Maneuvering Characteristics Augmentation System (MCAS), software designed to push the aircraft's nose down if it detected a stall during certain flight conditions. MCAS relied on information from a single angle-of-attack sensor, despite the aviation industry's established best practice of using redundant sensor sets (Shepardson & Rucinski, 2020).

In addition, Boeing's failure mode analyses and simulator tests underestimated the risk of erroneous sensor readings that triggered repeated nose-down commands. Pilots, trained on the assumption that the MAX cockpit behaved in much the same way as previous variants of the 737, had no clear procedures for ignoring MCAS failures. Corporate pressures to minimize additional pilot training and speed up production schedules had subtly deprioritized exhaustive engineering checks. The resulting tragedies forced regulators around the world to suspend the MAX fleet for almost two years and provoked a worrying reckoning about how schedule metrics and cost-saving targets can eclipse life-critical safety data.

In the automotive world, the *General Motors ignition switch defect* illustrates a different kind of data malpractice. Between 2005 and 2014, a latent defect in certain GM models allowed engines to stall during collisions, disabling airbags and power steering. Internal engineering failure records had flagged the problem as early as 2001, but GM's safety metrics measured only the costs of warranty claims and litigation payouts, both modest when the defect first appeared.

As a result, engineers and managers classified the first incidents as isolated anomalies rather than systemic design flaws. When the company finally issued a recall in 2014, it acknowledged that at least 124 lives had been lost (Shepardson, 2018). The tragedy highlighted how narrowly defined performance indicators, such as a decline in the number of recalls, can hide damage if they fail to capture raw incident data.

One last illustration comes from the field of *high-speed finance*. In August 2012, Knight Capital Group launched a new trading algorithm on the New York Stock Exchange. Within 45 minutes, the faulty code sent out millions of erroneous buy and sell orders, creating huge price swings in dozens of stocks.

Knight lost $440 million before the system could be stopped, losing so much and so quickly that it needed an emergency infusion of capital to avoid bankruptcy (Horowitz & Menn, 2012). The collapse, later attributed to a misconfigured code deployment process and insufficient testing before launch, epitomizes the principle of "garbage in, garbage out". Vast computing power and low-latency data feeds amplify small errors into catastrophic losses.

LESSONS LEARNED: PATTERNS AND PITFALLS

As we reflect on these cautionary tales, several recurring patterns, based on human and technical failings, become more evident.

First, *technical sophistication alone does not guarantee accuracy*. The Gaussian copula, MCAS software, AI diagnostic tools, and algorithmic trading mechanisms share a common vulnerability: they have treated historical or curated data as immutable truths, ignoring the possibility of variable correlations, sensor failures, unrepresentative training sets, and the complexity of the real world. Models remain as robust as their assumptions; when those assumptions break down, the most elaborate equations offer no refuge.

Second, *Goodhart's Law* holds true across industries. Whether sales quotas incentivize ghost accounts at Wells Fargo, late fees mask the appeal of Netflix subscriptions at Blockbuster, or recall reduction targets delay safety fixes at GM, the moment a metric becomes the sole focus of incentives, it invites gaming, redefinition, or outright fabrication. Metrics created to measure progress can turn into performance targets that distort behavior and erode the underlying goals.

Third, *organizational culture and cognitive biases* amplify blind spots. In NASA's culture of schedule pressure, engineers' concerns about sealing rings in cold climates were subordinated to the imperatives of the launch window. At Lehman Brothers and Goldman Sachs, traders fascinated by proven returns silenced doubts about counterparty risk. In government agencies, reporting structures that discouraged dissent led managers to inflate Soviet production figures or underestimate the danger of hurricanes. In all these examples, fear of career risk, deference to authority, and the collective desire to believe positive narratives overcame critical inquiry.

Finally, *ethical lapses* in data presentation cause lasting damage. Deliberate cherry-picking, shifting baselines, selective disclosures, and spurious correlations betray public trust so deeply that even subsequent transparent efforts struggle to gain traction. Once a company, institution, or government body is exposed for manipulating data, be it Purdue Pharma,

Theranos, VW, or Cambridge Analytica, all future statistics it publishes are greeted with suspicion.

FINAL THOUGHTS

In our data-obsessed age, the promise of Big Data and artificial intelligence is irresistible. Yet, without the bedrock of skepticism, ethics, and organizational humility, that same promise can metamorphose into a source of harm.

The tragedies recounted in this chapter—economic collapses, corporate bankruptcies, policy blunders, medical scandals, and engineering failures—share a common root: an overconfidence in data as an oracle, rather than as a tool requiring rigorous oversight. If we are to harness analytics for genuine progress rather than sow dreams that turn to dust, we must build systems and cultures that treat every statistic as provisional, every model as a hypothesis to be tested, and every forecast as an invitation to dissent.

Only then can data serve human values rather than subvert them—and only then can we avert the next disaster spawned by our own creation.

CHAPTER 11
FIXING THE PROBLEM

> *In a world of more data, the companies with more data-literate people are the ones that are going to win.*
>
> — MIRO KAZAKOFF

In previous chapters, we cataloged data-driven disasters: math that masqueraded as truth, data pipelines riddled with hidden errors, dashboards that fooled even the most experienced executives, models that adjusted for past noise rather than future realities, averages that obscured variability and metrics that were manipulated until they bore little resemblance to what they were intended to measure.

We explored how cognitive biases (our own mental shortcuts) further distort the way we collect, interpret, and present data. We saw that the root cause of these calamities rarely lies in the absence of data or technology, but in organizational cultures that value polished appearances over ruthless scrutiny, reward short-term gains over long-term resilience, and treat data as a totem rather than a tool.

In this chapter, we move from diagnosis to cure: we offer a practical and comprehensive guide to large-scale fixes for BI and data-driven decision-making, anchored in a *Bayesian mindset*, which regards every piece of evidence as provisional, every probability as subject to updating and every decision as an exercise in continuous learning, rather than following rigid rules.

Our approach unfolds in a series of eight interlinked steps. The first four steps address the core technical fundamentals: ensuring the integrity of data pipelines, redesigning dashboards to communicate uncertainty rather than false precision, automating validation and quality assurance, and inoculating models against overfitting.

Steps five and six rise to a higher plane of abstraction, encouraging organizations to adopt systems thinking and scenario planning when tackling complexity and to incorporate five organizational practices: peer review, hypothesis-driven analysis, rigorous documentation, cross-functional collaboration, and pilot testing, which guard against simplistic correlation traps.

The seventh stage addresses the human dimension: eliminating cognitive bias at scale through adversarial teams, data literacy training, and requirements for multiple independent lines of evidence. Finally, the eighth stage re-establishes trust in metrics by imposing transparent definitions, consistent standards, and external audits.

Throughout these eight steps, there is a common thread of Bayesian reasoning: we encourage stakeholders to treat each analytical insight as a hypothesis to be constantly revised in light of new data, to quantify uncertainty whenever possible, and to prefer probability distributions and confidence intervals over single-point estimates.

STEP 1: STRENGTHEN DATA PIPELINES TO AVOID "GARBAGE IN, GARBAGE OUT"

The most fundamental fix is at the very beginning of the analysis: the data pipeline. Too often, faulty inputs from external sources, such as customer surveys with biased sampling, sensors that drift over time, and financial reports compiled in outdated spreadsheets, enter BI systems without any real-time validation, while legacy platforms have no hooks to flag inconsistencies or schema changes.

The first imperative is to *treat data pipelines as mission-critical production systems*, complete with unit tests, continuous integration, and version-controlled schemas. Instead, organizations should adopt automated strategies, such as conditional imputation rules that are based on domain knowledge (such as pre-filling for telemetry flows, and model-based imputation for customer demographics) and, above all, should record each substitution instead of silently overwriting nulls.

In addition to imputation, *AI-driven anomaly detection tools* can examine incoming data for outliers or sudden changes in distribution, whether it be a sudden 40% drop in call volume or an impossible spike in sensor readings, and generate alerts for human reviewers. Pipeline architects must cross-check several independent sources, reconciling CRM data with billing records, comparing warehouse stock levels with ERP records, and correlating website analytics with CDN server records, before the data flows into marts and downstream dashboards.

Finally, the formation of dedicated *data governance teams* that carry out regular pipeline integrity audits, trace lineage, and enforce schema contracts ensures that by the time data reaches analysts, its provenance and integrity are no longer in doubt.

A vivid illustration of robust pipeline practices comes from NASA's real-time telemetry systems. During interplanetary missions, each spacecraft emits thousands of metrics per second, from gyroscopic stabilizers to thermal sensors. Engineers cannot tolerate a single bad reading triggering an erroneous thrust command or hiding a genuine anomaly.

To prevent junk telemetry from corrupting mission decisions, NASA employs three layers of defense: hardware-level checks that flag self-tests and sensor redundancies; firmware that filters out implausible values using statistical thresholds derived from historical baselines; and ground-based anomaly detection systems that continuously compare incoming data streams with predictive models (Morgan, n.d.).

When an anomalous spike appears, such as a sudden temperature reading hundreds of degrees outside the expected range, several team members receive immediate alerts, and a predefined "red team" analyzes the raw packets for data corruption before any automated response is executed. This regimented approach to pipeline integrity has allowed NASA to recover smoothly from sensor failures that would have been catastrophic in less disciplined environments.

STEP 2: REDESIGN BI DASHBOARDS TO MINIMIZE MISINTERPRETATION

Even perfect data can be misleading if it is displayed without context or nuance. Executives are prone to trusting dashboards too much, especially when they display shiny gauges and sharp numbers that convey a false sense of certainty.

As we've seen, dashboards often manipulate perception: overly precise statistics mask the underlying measurement error; truncated y-axes exaggerate small fluctuations, turning them into dramatic trends; and aggregated KPIs hide the full distribution of data. To counteract these tendencies, dashboards must be redesigned to *accept and display uncertainty* rather than hide it.

Confidence intervals or error bands should accompany all time series lines; numbers should be rounded to reflect the true resolution of the data collection process (for example, reporting 35,400 ± 120 site visits instead of 35,432, which is hyper-precise); and all visualizations should offer alternative views, such as segmented dashboards that break down totals by region, customer group or product line, and raw data tables that allow advanced users to do detailed analyses of granular counts.

Equally important is *executive training*: leaders must learn to approach dashboards with healthy skepticism, asking not only "What do these numbers show?" but also "What might they be hiding?" before making important resource commitments.

Netflix provides a convincing example of dashboard redesign in practice. In its early days, Netflix's internal analytics platform featured vanity metrics such as total hours streamed and user completion rates, which executives celebrated as proof of engagement. However, they soon realized that these metrics were disconnected from commercial value: they didn't predict subscription renewals or referral fees.

In response, Netflix's data team completely rebuilt the dashboard with a layered design. The top layer showed aggregate revenue per subscriber and retention groups. Hovering over any point revealed the distribution of engagement between content types. An optional "analysis mode" displayed standard deviations and interquartile ranges for each series, allowing content teams to see which shows had polarized audiences compared to broad appeal.

Because the dashboard presented user-level data in an anonymous and privacy-preserving way, product teams could explore niche segments, for example, 25 to 34 year-old sci-fi enthusiasts in Tokyo, and correlate their viewing patterns with the risk of abandonment. The result was a move away from fragile vanity metrics toward a metrics architecture that aligned closely with the long-term value of subscriber lifetime (Richwine & Chmielewski, 2024).

STEP 3: AUTOMATE DATA VALIDATION AND QUALITY ASSURANCE

While improvements in the data pipeline detect many problems upstream, organizations should also assume that no data arrives perfectly clean. In most traditional BI systems, data is ingested, polished, and then deemed reliable, only to propagate errors in reports and models.

To break this chain, companies must implement *real-time data validation tools* that intercept anomalies before they taint reports. Validators based on machine learning can be trained on historical data to recognize normal patterns, such as daily transaction volumes or sensor deviations within known limits, and flag any deviations beyond a dynamically calculated threshold.

Complementing these AI tools, a set of *statistical sanity checks*, such as Benford's Law tests for first-digit distributions or autocorrelation analyses for seasonal patterns, can automatically highlight suspicious trends or flat series.

An additional layer of defense involves *independent data verification*: periodically comparing internal metrics with external sources, such as industry averages, peer performance, or syndicated data sets. By overlaying an internal sales curve with publicly disclosed market growth rates, for example, a company can confirm that its own growth is within a plausible range. When discrepancies arise, for example, internal sales increasing by 50% in a market that is officially contracting, investigations can reveal everything from missing currency conversions to deliberate misreporting.

Hedge funds have been among the pioneers of real-time anomaly detection, precisely because even a single incorrect data point can wreak havoc on algorithmic trading models. Companies like Two Sigma and Quantitative Risk Management (QRM) instrument their data sources with "guardrails" that constantly monitor price quotes, volume spikes, and order book imbalances.

When an incoming tick deviates by more than a statistically determined number of standard deviations from recent trends, or when correlated instruments diverge unexpectedly, the system automatically limits trading activity and sends alerts to the human supervision teams. This proactive stance prevents models from executing trades based on phantom prices or reacting to rapid failures, and has become a gold standard for risk-sensitive organizations (Singh, 2025).

STEP 4: PREVENT OVERFITTING AND FALSE PATTERNS IN DATA MODELS

Complex machine learning models are powerful but dangerously prone to overfitting, learning all the peculiarities of the training data, including random noise, rather than robust, generalizable relationships.

To avoid this situation, organizations should *favor simpler, more interpretable algorithms* whenever possible, reserving deep neural networks or ensemble methods for problems where their advantages justify the added complexity. Most importantly, all models should be subjected to rigorous endurance tests on datasets that have never been seen during training, including splits out of time (such as training on data up to 2019 and testing in 2020-2021) to simulate evolving conditions.

The commitment to *adaptive learning* ensures that the models detect changes in distribution, for example, in consumer behavior or market volatility, and are trained or recalibrated automatically when performance declines.

Google's approach to detecting fraud in its advertising network is an excellent example. Instead of implementing an impenetrable black box model, Google's security team creates transparent, rule-based classifiers that flag known fraud patterns, complemented by simpler gradient-boost models that ingest aggregate characteristics such as click speed, device type, and geographic behavior.

The predictions of each model are monitored in production, and when there is a sudden increase in false positives or negatives, often due to fraudsters changing tactics, an automatic alert triggers a manual analysis. As the models are modular and interpretable, engineers can quickly isolate which feature sets have deviated, inject new examples into the training pipeline, and restore forecast accuracy in a few hours rather than weeks (Sculley et al., 2011).

STEP 5: DEALING WITH COMPLEXITY—SYSTEMS THINKING AND SCENARIO PLANNING

Despite our best modeling efforts, reality rarely conforms to correlations of two variables. Business cycles, consumer sentiment, and operational efficiency emerge from complex networks of interconnected factors.

Adopting *systems thinking* means mapping these networks, identifying feedback loops, time lags, and external factors, before drawing conclusions from the data. A systemic approach can reveal, for example, that a correlation between the frequency of use of a product and customer retention is the result of a triangular network: frequency of use increases with social referrals, referrals increase due to a marketing campaign, and retention responds to both use and the strength of social proof. Only by mapping this system can teams create interventions such as increasing referrals through specific incentives, rather than chasing the illusion that usage alone determines loyalty.

When environments are volatile, *scenario planning* complements systems thinking by predicting several futures. Instead of endorsing a single narrative ("increased advertising spending will increase sales"), organizations develop a set of plausible scenarios: one in which the launch of a competitor reduces returns, another in which supply chain constraints strangle compliance, and a third in which economic headwinds squeeze consumer spending.

For each scenario, the teams specify the key indicators, test the models, and define contingency plans. This method guards against simplistic correlation traps, where a single observed pattern generates a one-size-fits-all strategy, incorporating organizational flexibility in decision-making.

STEP 6: ORGANIZATIONAL PRACTICES THAT PREVENT CORRELATION TRAPS

To translate conceptual knowledge into daily discipline, organizations must adopt three fundamental practices.

First, *regular peer review of knowledge*: teams should present their findings to colleagues outside their domain, inviting new perspectives that may detect confusing variables or reverse causes. Second, hypothesis-driven analysis: every deep dive starts with a clearly articulated hypothesis; unexpected correlations become hypotheses for further investigation, not immediate action items.

Third, *documented methodology*: all data sources, transformations, and statistical techniques are recorded in a central repository, ensuring transparency and allowing others to replicate or challenge the work. Fourth, cross-functional collaboration: marketing, finance, operations, and technology all take part in formulating questions and interpreting the results, enriching the analysis with expertise from different fields.

Finally, *pilot programs or small-scale tests*: when insights suggest a major strategic change, teams carry out controlled experiments, whether it's an A/B test on a subset of customers or a limited production ramp-up, to validate causal hypotheses before reallocating resources widely.

Each of these practices embodies a Bayesian mindset: by treating initial knowledge as provisional, subjecting it to the scrutiny of various experts, and validating it through small-scale experiments, organizations continually update their collective convictions in a disciplined way. Over time, this fosters a culture in which data-driven decisions evolve through iterative refinement rather than one-off proclamations.

STEP 7: ELIMINATE COGNITIVE BIAS FROM DECISION MAKING AT SCALE

Technical corrections alone cannot eliminate the distortions of our own minds. Cognitive biases such as confirmation bias, anchoring bias, and availability bias, insidiously infiltrate BI tools and decision-making processes.

To protect against these biases, organizations can form dedicated *"red teams"* whose sole purpose is to challenge prevailing interpretations before strategic commitments are made. Data literacy training programs should include modules on common biases, teaching analysts and executives to recognize, for example, why confirming evidence appears more persuasive than data that does not.

In addition, teams should be required to *justify major decisions* using several independent data sets, never relying on a single report, and to document the alternative explanations that were considered and discarded. By institutionalizing disagreement and demanding transparency about decision-making criteria, companies reduce the risk that biases in the design of the dashboard, the choice of model, or the framing of metrics will steer them toward non-optimal strategies.

Amazon's famous "disagree and commit" culture offers a practical example. When a team proposes a major initiative based on BI insights, other leaders are explicitly tasked with disagreeing, presenting counterarguments, and pointing out contradictory data. Only after these objections have been addressed does the organization commit to a course of action. This ritualized tension between conviction and skepticism ensures that cognitive biases are revealed early on, that decisions are based on a more balanced evidence base, and that dissenting voices are heard without hindering progress.

STEP 8: CREATING TRANSPARENT AND RELIABLE METRICS

Even the best technical and cultural fixes will fail if the metrics themselves lack integrity. To regain trust, organizations must define clear and consistent standards for each essential metric. What exactly constitutes an "active user"? Should it be a login, a transaction, or an event in the application? Who decides?

The answers should be in a version-controlled *Metric Registry*, with immutable definitions once published and change requests subject to review by a cross-functional committee. Any change to the formula of a metric must be accompanied by a public record of changes, explaining the justification, the expected impact, and the effective date.

In the case of externally reported metrics, such as financial results, public health statistics, or environmental indicators, *independent audits* should verify not only the numbers but also the methodologies. In regulated sectors, organizations should treat this disclosure as a compliance requirement and a strategic asset: transparency generates credibility with investors, regulators, and the public.

The U.S. Securities and Exchange Commission's crackdown on "non-GAAP" financial measures illustrates the power of regulation to curb the manipulation of metrics. By requiring companies to reconcile adjusted earnings with standardized GAAP figures and explain each adjustment, regulators have reduced the proliferation of creative accounting practices and restored comparability between companies (SEC, 2023). Similar principles apply to BI: each adjusted KPI is juxtaposed with its unadjusted counterpart, each seasonal adjustment is documented, and each outlier removal is disclosed.

EMBRACING A BAYESIAN FUTURE

BI is not about static rules or immutable dashboards. It is a process of perpetual updating: new data arrives, models are refined, and beliefs are revised. A Bayesian mindset is the basis for each of the eight steps described above. By strengthening pipelines, we continually update our confidence in data sources; by redesigning dashboards, we communicate the evolution of uncertainties; by automating validation, we refine our assumptions about what is "normal"; by avoiding overfitting, we penalize model complexity that does not survive out-of-sample testing.

In systems thinking and scenario planning, we assign probabilities to various futures; in organizational practices, we treat analyses as hypotheses to be tested; in bias mitigation, we combine evidence from several independent data sets; and in metrics governance, we version control and revise definitions in light of new requirements.

Adopting Bayesian practices requires technical skill and cultural humility. Organizations must normalize the language of uncertainty: point estimates become distributions, confidence intervals are shown on every graph, and leaders learn to ask "How sure are we?" instead of demanding "What's the best number?" This change dissolves the allure of false precision and transforms data-driven decision-making into a continuously improving dialogue between evidence and judgment.

OVERCOMING IMPLEMENTATION CHALLENGES

Implementing these fixes on a large scale is undoubtedly a challenge. Legacy systems resist change, departmental silos accumulate data instead of sharing it, and executives accustomed to bullet-point recommendations may refuse to accept nuanced probability presentations.

Overcoming these barriers requires ongoing leadership commitment: executive board sponsors must *publicly champion new practices, allocate budgets for data infrastructure modernization, and embed BI governance at the highest levels of corporate policy.* Training programs should improve the skills not only of data scientists, but also of all stakeholders who consume analytics: finance, marketing, operations, legal, and human resources. Performance evaluations should reward behaviors that reveal data problems early, invite criticism of polished dashboards, and encourage exploration of alternative scenarios.

In addition, technology platforms must be updated. Modern data catalogs, lineage tools, and observability frameworks make it much easier to track pipeline integrity, monitor model performance deviations, and apply metric definitions. Cloud-based BI platforms support interactive dashboards with built-in uncertainty visualization. Integrated DevOps pipelines can treat data processing code with the same rigor as application code, with automated testing and version control. While these investments require time and resources, the alternative—repeated data-driven disasters—proves far costlier.

FINAL THOUGHTS

The promise of data-driven innovation remains immense: more precise allocation of resources, faster discovery of insights, and the possibility of an evidence-based strategy that overcomes intuition. However, as we have seen, these benefits only materialize in a broader ecosystem of technical rigor, ethical discipline, and cultural humility. The eight steps described in this chapter collectively raise the bar for organizational capability, minimizing the risk of catastrophic failure and allowing teams to learn, adapt, and make better decisions under uncertainty.

Ultimately, fixing the problem is not a one-off program, but an ongoing continuous improvement. A data-resilient organization is one that never stops asking questions: Are our pipelines healthy? Do our dashboards reflect true uncertainty? Are our models still valid? What new evidence has emerged? Are we inadvertently rewarding the wrong metrics? By institutionalizing a Bayesian approach, treating every insight as tentative, every decision as subject to revision, and every metric as a hypothesis to be tested, organizations transform BI from a static set of reports into a dynamic feedback loop that grows stronger with each iteration.

FIXING THE PROBLEM 191

Our hope is that the lessons and prescriptions in this chapter will serve as a springboard for transformation. The path may be challenging, but the prize is a culture in which data actually generates better results rather than misleads.

May your pipelines remain pure, your dashboards honest, your models robust, your scenarios broad, your teams skeptical, and your metrics always transparent. In this spirit, we will embrace the art of continuous updating and create analytical ecosystems that serve human values rather than subvert them. In our final chapter, we will look at the *future of decision-making*, exploring how real-time intelligence and AI-enhanced judgment will redefine what it means to be truly data-driven.

CHAPTER 12
THE FUTURE OF DECISION-MAKING

> *We are moving slowly into an era where Big Data is the starting point, not the end.*
>
> — PEARL ZHU

As we stand on the threshold of a new era in organizational decision-making, it seems that tools and techniques once reserved for science fiction are fast becoming a reality in everyday life. Decisions that once required weeks of data collection, analysis, and debate can now be informed in real time by machine learning algorithms, cloud-based analytics platforms, and seamless integrations between global data streams.

However, despite all the promises of speed and scale, a profound question arises: in a world where machines can process orders of magnitude more information than any human being could imagine, how can we ensure that these decisions remain anchored in purpose, ethics, and critical judgment?

This chapter explores how BI and artificial intelligence (AI) are reshaping the decision-making landscape, looks at the emerging technologies on the horizon, examines the evolving regulatory and ethical frameworks, and, most importantly, articulates why the irreplaceable capacity of human critical thinking will remain the cornerstone of sound decisions for decades to come.

FROM HUMAN-DRIVEN DECISIONS TO AI-DRIVEN DECISIONS

For much of the 20th century, decision-making in organizations followed a predictable rhythm: information was meticulously collected, compiled into monthly or quarterly reports, presented in boardrooms, and debated before any course corrections were implemented. Speed was limited by the constraints of manual data entry, batch processing, and paper governance.

But the turn of the millennium introduced a seismic shift. Enterprise resource planning systems, along with the emergence of cloud computing, enabled continuous data flows instead of static snapshots. With the advent of machine learning, organizations were able to start exploring large amounts of structured and unstructured data, discovering patterns that eluded traditional statistical methods.

Today, many leading companies operate decision cycles that are more like control systems than static planning cycles. Sensors embedded in manufacturing equipment transmit performance metrics to centralized analysis mechanisms that detect incipient equipment failures before they occur. Customer interactions on web, mobile, and in-store channels feed recommendation engines that adjust marketing offers in real time.

Even in high-risk environments such as financial trading or emergency response, AI-driven systems can process news feeds, social media sentiment, and market fluctuations in milliseconds, flagging anomalies and suggesting responses long before a human operator can analyze the details.

However, this transformation does not make human decision-makers obsolete. On the contrary, it *redefines* their role. Machines excel at ingesting, filtering, and correlating large volumes of data; humans retain the unique faculties of moral reasoning, strategic vision, and contextual understanding.

The future will reward organizations that design decision-making ecosystems in which AI takes care of the heavy lifting of data processing, while humans focus on interpreting the results, defining strategic priorities, and ensuring alignment with organizational values and long-term goals.

This "human-in-the-loop" paradigm is what will be needed for effective and responsible AI-driven decision-making.

THE POWER OF PREDICTIVE ANALYTICS

One of the most profound advances in recent years has been the maturation of predictive analytics, which has gone from an academic novelty to an operational necessity. Unlike descriptive analysis, which analyzes the past to explain what happened, predictive analysis uses historical data and sophisticated algorithms to predict what is likely to happen next.

In retail, for example, predictive models analyze purchase histories, website behavior, weather patterns, and even social media trends to forecast demand down to the SKU level. Inventory managers can then adjust stocking decisions with unprecedented precision, minimizing stock-outs without incurring excessive transportation costs.

In finance, machine learning-enabled credit risk models ingest thousands of variables, from transaction histories and macroeconomic indicators to real-time social sentiment, to predict defaults weeks or months before they materialize. Lenders can proactively engage at-risk customers with customized refinancing options or dynamically adjust lending criteria in market environments.

In the healthcare sector, predictive algorithms examine electronic health records, genetic information, and population health trends to identify patients at risk of chronic diseases, enabling early interventions that reduce hospitalizations and improve outcomes.

However, the full power of predictive analytics only comes when organizations adopt a culture of continuous model validation and recalibration. Predictive models, like any statistical approach, depend on assumptions about the stability of patterns. Market disruptions, regulatory changes, and unforeseen events (such as global pandemics) can render even the most advanced models obsolete.

Future-proof companies institute rigorous out-of-sample testing, scenario-based stress tests, and automated monitoring of model performance in real environments. When predictions fail, rapid retraining protocols ensure that analysis pipelines adapt without compromising the reliability of operational decisions.

THE RISE OF AI DASHBOARDS

As predictive analytics becomes an integral part of daily operations, the interface through which insights reach decision-makers needs to evolve. The static, spreadsheet-driven dashboards of the past cannot keep up with the demands of real-time intelligence. In their place, AI-powered dashboards are emerging: interactive, self-updating screens that not only display metrics but also interpret them, highlight anomalies, and present root cause analyses on demand.

Consider a supply chain control tower dashboard that integrates streaming data from IoT sensors on a global fleet of vessels, production schedules from different factories, and real-time demand signals from point-of-sale systems. When transit delays threaten key components, the AI layer flags the event, correlates it with port congestion and weather forecasts, and generates a prioritized list of mitigation strategies, such as rerouting via alternative carriers, rebalancing stock buffers, or shipping critical consignments by air freight. Decision-makers can dig deeper into each recommendation, visualize the supporting data, and override the automated suggestions if broader strategic considerations warrant it.

These AI dashboards combine natural language summaries with visual analysis. Instead of manually interpreting a dozen graphs, leaders can ask, "What are our top three supply chain risks this week?" and receive concise, plain-language briefings, complemented by links to detailed data visualizations. By incorporating explainable AI techniques, showing which factors contributed most to a flagged risk, the dashboards build trust and empower users to make informed decisions quickly.

However, the move to AI dashboards requires careful *UX design*. Overloading users with alerts can lead to fatigue, while hiding critical swathes of uncertainty can promote misplaced trust. The most effective AI dashboards strike a balance between automation and human oversight, displaying only high-value alerts, allowing interactive exploration of key factors, and always providing transparent explanations of the underlying analysis.

FACING THE "BLACK BOX" CHALLENGE

Despite their power, many machine learning models remain opaque "black boxes," especially deep neural networks that process inputs through layers of non-linear transformations. For organizations operating in regulated industries or making high-risk decisions such as credit approvals, medical diagnoses, and personnel evaluations, the inscrutability of these models is a significant obstacle. Stakeholders require accurate predictions and clear rationales: how and why did the model come to this conclusion?

To meet this challenge, the field of *explainable AI (XAI)* has matured rapidly. Techniques such as *SHAP (Shapley additive explanations) and LIME (local interpretable model-agnostic explanations)* quantify the contribution of each input resource to a given prediction. The generation of counterfactuals demonstrates how small adjustments to the input data would alter the model's results, clarifying critical sensitivities. Model-specific methods, such as attention map visualization in transformative models, highlight the textual or visual elements that guided classification decisions.

Organizations that integrate XAI into their decision-making workflows can associate each AI recommendation with an intelligible explanation: "We flagged this invoice as potentially fraudulent because it deviates significantly from your historical payment patterns, both in terms of timing and supplier geography." This transparency promotes trust, encourages human users to engage critically with AI results, and reduces the risk of uncontrolled automation.

However, XAI is not a panacea. The explanations themselves can be misleading if not carefully validated, and some high-dimensional models resist direct interpretation. The most robust approach combines XAI techniques with human-in-the-loop review processes: AI provides hypotheses and explanations, while domain experts validate, refine, and, where necessary, override the model's recommendations to ensure that decisions remain grounded in real-world context and ethical considerations.

PROTECTING AGAINST BIAS AND ENSURING FAIRNESS

Along with the imperative of transparency, organizations have to face the risk of algorithmic bias. Machine learning models learn from historical data, which often reflects systemic inequalities based on race, gender, socioeconomic status, or geography. In lending, sentencing algorithms, and hiring platforms, these biases have the potential to perpetuate or amplify discrimination at scale.

The future of decision-making requires that fairness be a first-class performance criterion. This starts with *diverse and representative training data*. Data collection processes must be audited for completeness and balance, ensuring that underrepresented groups are neither ignored nor stereotyped. Feature selection methodologies should exclude proxies for protected attributes, and deviation algorithms such as reweighting schemes, adversarial deviations, or optimization with equity constraints should be incorporated into model training pipelines.

Equally important is the *continuous monitoring of fairness*. Predictive models should be regularly evaluated for disparate impact metrics: false positive and false negative rates in protected groups, demographic parity, and equal probabilities. When systemic bias arises, organizations need protocols for quickly retraining the model, adjusting thresholds, or, in extreme cases, temporarily suspending automated decisions until the problems are resolved.

The creation and operation of these equity structures by design require *interdisciplinary collaboration*. Data scientists, legal experts, ethicists, and representatives of the affected communities must be involved in the verification and governance processes of the models. By incorporating diverse perspectives at the heart of AI projects, organizations can mitigate biases and foster trust among stakeholders who might otherwise view automated decision-making with skepticism.

THE FUTURE OF DECISION-MAKING 201

THE ESSENTIAL ROLE OF HUMAN JUDGMENT

Despite the rise of AI and automation, human judgment will continue to be indispensable for navigating the moral and strategic aspects of decision-making that machines cannot replicate. While algorithms excel at pattern recognition and optimization within well-defined parameters, humans have the capacity for holistic reasoning, empathy, and long-term vision.

In clinical contexts, for example, diagnostic support systems analyze medical images and patient history to suggest likely conditions. However, only a doctor can integrate a patient's unique preferences, psychosocial context, and comorbidities into a patient-centered care plan. In supply chain management, AI can recommend the most cost-effective routing of goods, but only experienced supply chain leaders can weigh up factors such as geopolitical risks, supplier relationships, and corporate sustainability commitments.

To ensure that AI augments and does not replace human judgment, organizations must design decision-making processes that assign authority appropriately. High-confidence, low-risk decisions, such as automatically ordering low-value office supplies, can be fully delegated to automation.

Crucial decisions with legal, ethical, or reputational implications, such as hiring, compliance exceptions, or crisis management, should always involve a human checkpoint. In addition, training programs should emphasize critical thinking skills: the ability to question model assumptions, investigate alternative hypotheses, and balance quantitative results with qualitative knowledge.

By consciously delineating the spheres of machine efficiency and human insight, companies can harness the best of both worlds: the relentless speed and scale of AI, along with the wisdom, creativity, and ethical compass that only humans can provide.

CULTIVATING CRITICAL THINKING AND DATA LITERACY

We've already discussed this, but here's a reminder that as AI and advanced analytics penetrate all functions, data literacy becomes not only a competitive advantage but also a fundamental skill for all employees. The company of the future expects leaders at all levels to understand the basic concepts of probability, statistics, and causal inference. They must feel comfortable interpreting confidence intervals, recognizing the difference between correlation and causation, and questioning the assumptions built into predictive models.

To achieve this, organizations will invest heavily in comprehensive data literacy programs. These include interactive workshops on statistical reasoning, immersive simulations that expose participants to common cognitive biases, and scenario-based exercises in which cross-functional teams design and critique analytical workflows. Data science champions as analysts and engineers fluent in both technical rigor and business context will guide colleagues in real-world projects, translating abstract analytical concepts into practical knowledge.

In addition, a culture of constructive skepticism must be fostered. Employees should feel empowered to question model results without fear of reprisal, present alternative explanations for emerging trends, and demand proof before committing resources. By institutionalizing "pre-mortems", in which teams imagine potential failures of AI-driven initiatives and brainstorm countermeasures, organizations can inoculate themselves against overconfidence and groupthink.

Ultimately, a truly data-literate workforce turns analysis from a closed function into a collective competence. When all stakeholders, from first-line managers to top executives, can meaningfully engage with data, decision-making becomes richer, more inclusive, and more resilient.

DECISION-MAKING BEYOND AI: QUANTUM COMPUTING AND DECENTRALIZATION

Looking beyond the horizon of current AI and cloud architectures, two emerging paradigms promise to reshape decision-making in profound ways.

The first is ,. Although still in their infancy, quantum processors have the potential to solve certain classes of combinatorial optimization and simulation problems much more efficiently than classical machines. In logistics, quantum-enhanced algorithms could evaluate billions of routing permutations in real time, dynamically re-optimizing global supply networks in relation to disruptions, capacity constraints, and changes in demand. In materials science, quantum simulations could reveal complex molecular interactions, accelerating the discovery of new compounds for pharmaceuticals, energy storage, and carbon capture.

Organizations that start exploring hybrid classical and quantum workflows today by modernizing data architectures, cultivating quantum-savvy talent, and prototyping pilot applications will be well placed to reap the rewards as hardware resources mature. However, quantum computing also brings new challenges for data security, as quantum-safe cryptographic standards become necessary to protect sensitive decision pipelines.

The second frontier is *decentralization through distributed recording technologies*. Traditional BI systems rely on centralized data warehouses and data lakes that can become single points of failure or control. Blockchain and related architectures enable peer-to-peer networks in which data provenance is immutable, access is governed by smart contracts,, and trust is established through cryptographic consensus rather than centralized authorities.

In trade finance, for example, a consortium of banks, carriers, and customs authorities could share a unified record of shipping documents, reducing fraud and speeding up the settlement of transactions. In environmental monitoring, decentralized sensor networks could record emissions data transparently, enabling regulators, NGOs and citizens to verify corporate sustainability statements in real time.

While decentralization increases transparency and resilience, it also requires new governance models. Organizations need to navigate the trade-offs between openness and data privacy, reconcile jurisdictional regulations, and design incentive structures that align different stakeholders toward common decision outcomes.

PREPARING FOR THE FUTURE: ORGANIZATIONAL ADAPTATION

To thrive in this evolving landscape, organizations must carry out deliberate adaptation on several fronts. First, they must develop *comprehensive AI and analytics roadmaps* that assess current capabilities, test emerging technologies,, and integrate new skills into talent strategies. This includes establishing centers of excellence for AI, embedding data scientists alongside domain experts, and fostering partnerships with academic institutions and technology providers.

Secondly, *ethical governance* must become an integral part of the analytics lifecycle. Cross-functional AI ethics boards, made up of data scientists, legal experts, ethicists, and external consultants, should evaluate proposed AI applications for fairness, transparency, and social impact before deployment. Policies for responsible AI implementation should codify best practices for bias mitigation, explainability, and human oversight in the loop, ensuring that ethical considerations are not afterthoughts but design principles.

Third, *compliance processes* must move from retrospective audits to real-time, policy-driven controls. Automated monitoring tools can flag potential violations of data privacy regulations, insider trading rules, or environmental standards as they occur, allowing for rapid remediation. By incorporating compliance protections directly into analysis pipelines, organizations can reduce risks while preserving agility.

Fourthly, *team structures* must evolve to break down traditional silos. Cross-functional squads that bring together data engineers, analysts, product managers, and subject matter experts can accelerate the implementation of AI-driven solutions while ensuring that technical excellence remains grounded in the operational context. Agile methodologies adapted to analytics, which include iterative experimentation, rapid prototyping, and continuous validation, replace monolithic project cycles with dynamic sprints that deliver incremental value.

Finally, leaders must adopt a *mindset of continuous learning*. Regular "analytical retrospectives" identify what worked and what failed, not only in technical implementation, but also in user adoption, ethical governance, and business results. Failure, when it occurs, is treated as a data point rather than a stigma, feeding into adjustments to models, processes, and training programs. By codifying these feedback loops, organizations turn learning into a strategic resource that adapts as quickly as the data landscape itself.

FINAL THOUGHTS

The future of decision-making lies not in the total replacement of human insight by machine automation, but in a deeper collaboration between human judgment and artificial intelligence. Data streams of unprecedented volume and speed will enable organizations to detect emerging risks, seize fleeting opportunities, and optimize operations on scales previously unimaginable. Predictive analytics, AI dashboards, and explainable models will become commonplace, while emerging quantum computing and decentralized architectures promise even more radical advances.

However, despite all the technological marvels on the horizon, the enduring essence of good decision-making will remain the same: the capacity for *critical thinking, ethical reasoning, and long-term vision*. Machines can reveal patterns and quantify probabilities, but only human beings can integrate context, weigh up competing values, and align decisions with a broader goal. Cultivating data literacy, incorporating human protections into the loop, institutionalizing ethical governance, and fostering a culture of constructive skepticism will ensure that AI amplifies, rather than erodes, human agency.

As we go through this transition, organizations that balance machine speed with human wisdom will achieve not only superior performance but also lasting trust. In a world full of data, the greatest competitive advantage will belong to those who remember that numbers serve human purposes, not the other way around. By embracing the art of continuous updating where every insight is provisional, every model is a hypothesis to be tested, and every decision is a chance to learn, we can unlock a future of faster, smarter, and profoundly more human decision-making.

CONCLUSION

As we come to the end of our apprenticeship through the hidden traps of BI, it's worth pausing to consider how far we've come—and how far we still have to go.

We began by confronting the seductive veneer of precision, witnessing how the mere glitter of decimal places can lull us into complacency. From there, we unearthed the fragility of our most elaborate data pipelines, only to discover that flawed inputs inevitably lead to flawed outputs.

We learned that apparent patterns can deceive us and that even the most advanced algorithms can be led astray by the randomness they mistake for signals. We saw how our dashboards, the modern altars of perception, can become instruments of distortion when their design obscures nuance, and how the metrics we hold most dear can be bent, reframed, or manipulated until they bear little resemblance to the truths they once sought to capture.

At the heart of our exploration was the human mind itself, with its predispositions toward ease and convenience: leaning toward familiar narratives, anchoring ourselves in first impressions, and favoring the comforting glow of confirming evidence. We confronted the ethical quagmires that arise when the lines between honest interpretation and deliberate manipulation become blurred, and we relied on real examples of ambition and arrogance gone wrong. On every occasion, the disaster stories reminded us that risks are not abstract; they are measured in lost fortunes, destroyed reputations, and the very human costs of misguided policy or medical errors.

However, this has never been a story of doom without promise. In our penultimate chapter, we outlined a way forward: strengthen pipelines with automated validation, redesign dashboards to accept uncertainty, vaccinate our models against overfitting, and integrate systems thinking and scenario planning into the fabric of organizational life. We have adopted a Bayesian mentality, which considers every prediction as provisional, every number as a hypothesis to be tested based on new evidence, and every decision as an invitation to learn.

Now, as this book takes its final bow, I invite you to *take these lessons beyond the page*. At your next strategy meeting, question the rounding conventions used to justify a gain from one quarter to the next. When a new forecasting model promises perfect accuracy, make sure its creators have tested it on truly unprecedented data. When a dashboard shows a reassuring trend, remember that behind its elegant visuals are assumptions that deserve scrutiny. Ask for provenance, demand transparency, and cultivate the habit of challenging your own intuitions. It is in these modest acts, these daily commitments to integrity and curiosity, that we transform the promise of data into genuine progress.

Looking to the future, the decision-making landscape will become increasingly complex. Real-time analytics will merge seamlessly with autonomous systems; quantum computing may one day analyze data we can't yet imagine, and AI-based knowledge will proliferate across all functions. And yet, in this glut of information, the essential question remains: can we still discern what matters from what merely dazzles? Will we build analytical ecosystems that amplify human values such as empathy, justice, and creativity, or will we allow algorithms to deepen our blind spots? The future will belong to those who recognize that technology can enhance, but not replace, the uniquely human capacities of judgment, skepticism, and moral reasoning.

If there's one conclusion I hope you take forward, it's this: the best decision-makers are neither those who bow unquestioningly at the altar of data, nor those who reject it completely in favor of instinct. Instead, they are those who stand at the intersection of perception and research, who treat every statistic as a starting point for conversation, every dashboard as a work in progress, and every predictive model as a reminder of our shared responsibility to ask "why" and "what if" before "how many".

Thank you for joining me in this exploration of BI's bright promise and darker shadows. If this book has raised your awareness, inspired a healthier skepticism, or armed you with concrete practices to improve your organization's analytics, I'd be grateful if you'd share your thoughts in a review on Amazon, Goodreads, or anywhere else thoughtful readers look for guidance. Your feedback not only helps others find the book, but it also sends a signal that the rigorous and ethical use of data is a priority worth defending.

At the end of the day, data is neither our savior nor our enemy; it is what we make of it. May you use it wisely, and may your decisions, informed by numbers and nuances, shape a future as enlightened as the analysis that guides it.

GLOSSARY

- **Anomaly detection:** Statistical or machine learning techniques that monitor incoming data streams to detect points, patterns, or changes that deviate markedly from established norms, triggering alerts for human review and preventing corrupt or fraudulent inputs from distorting downstream analysis.
- **Bayesian mindset:** A probabilistic framework that treats each insight as provisional, continually updating beliefs and predictions as new evidence emerges; it prioritizes the quantification of uncertainty over single-point estimates and promotes an iterative learning process in data-driven decision making.
- **Cognitive bias:** Systematic mental shortcuts - such as confirmation bias, anchoring, or availability heuristics that distort our perception of data, cause us to ignore contradictory evidence, and lead to overconfident or misinformed conclusions, unless they are proactively combated.
- **Confidence interval:** A statistical interval derived from sample data that expresses the degree of uncertainty around an estimate, indicating the range of values within which the true parameter probably

falls, reminding us that every number has an associated margin of error.
- **Correlation vs. causality:** The distinction between two variables that move together (correlation) and one variable that produces an effect on another (causality); understanding that high correlation can arise from coincidence or shared confounding factors, and never implies direct causation without further investigation.
- **Cross-validation:** A model evaluation technique that splits data into training and testing subsets multiple times to evaluate predictive performance on unseen samples, guarding against overfitting by ensuring that the apparent accuracy of a model is maintained beyond its original dataset.
- **Data governance:** A structure of policies, roles, responsibilities, and processes that guarantees the integrity, consistency, and security of data in an organization, including cataloguing definitions, controlling access, and maintaining audit trails for every transformation and metric change.
- **Data pipeline:** The end-to-end architecture, including data ingestion, cleansing, transformation, storage, and deliver, that powers analytics platforms; robust pipelines are treated like mission-critical software, with automated validation checks and real-time monitoring to detect errors early.
- **Data provenance:** The documented lineage of data, from its original source to each stage of processing, transformation, and aggregation, providing transparency about how each number was derived

and enabling audits, troubleshooting, and confidence in the insights reported.
- **GIGO (Garbage In, Garbage Out):** A principle that warns that flawed, incomplete, or biased inputs inevitably produce flawed outputs, regardless of analytical sophistication, emphasizing the fundamental importance of upstream data quality and rigorous validation before drawing conclusions.
- **Human-in-the-loop:** An approach that integrates supervision or manual intervention at key stages of automated workflows, such as model training, anomaly review, or decision approval, to combine computational speed with human judgment, context, and ethical consideration.
- **Key performance indicator (KPI):** A quantifiable measure selected to assess an organization's performance against strategic objectives; KPIs should be clearly defined, version-controlled, and accompanied by provenance and warnings to avoid unintentional definition changes or gaming.
- **Overfitting:** A modeling trap in which an algorithm captures random noise or quirks from historical data instead of underlying patterns, resulting in excellent in-sample accuracy but poor generalization to new real-world data.
- **Predictive analysis:** Techniques that take advantage of statistical models and machine learning to predict future results or trends based on historical and real-time data, enabling proactive decision-making, but they are only as reliable as the inputs, assumptions, and validation processes that support them.

- **Self-updating reports:** Dashboards or analytics that update automatically based on live data feeds - powerful for timeliness, but dangerous if users assume the numbers are infallible; they require built-in validation, version history, and clear flags for incomplete or anomalous entries.
- **Transparency:** The discipline of openly disclosing data sources, methodology, metric definitions, transformation steps, and known limitations alongside each report or dashboard - empowering stakeholders to interpret the results accurately and challenge possible distortions.
- **Vanity metrics:** Impressive but ultimately superficial measures (such as download counts, page views, social media "likes") that can convey popularity without revealing true value or business impact, diverting attention from more actionable metrics such as retention rates or customer lifetime value.
- **Version control:** The practice of tracking and managing changes to data schemas, transformation scripts, metric definitions, and analytical code, ensuring that all modifications are time-stamped, documented, and reversible, thus avoiding silent changes to reported figures.

REFERENCES

Armstrong, Z., & Wattenberg, M. (2014). Visualizing statistical mix effects and Simpson's paradox. *IEEE Transactions on Visualization and Computer Graphics,* 20(12), 2132–2141. https://doi.org/10.1109/tvcg.2014.2346297

Arthur, C. (2014, March 27). *Google flu trends is no longer good at predicting flu, scientists find.* The Guardian. https://www.theguardian.com/technology/2014/mar/27/google-flu-trends-predicting-flu

Barr, A. (2013, June 18). *From the ashes of Webvan, Amazon builds a grocery business.* Reuters. https://www.reuters.com/article/technology/from-the-ashes-of-webvan-amazon-builds-a-grocery-business-idUSBRE95H1CC/

Bilton, N. (2016, September 6). *Exclusive: How Elizabeth Holmes's House of Cards Came tumbling down.* Vanity Fair. https://www.vanityfair.com/news/2016/09/elizabeth-holmes-theranos-exclusive

Chong, C. (2015, July 17). *Blockbuster's CEO once passed up a chance to buy Netflix for only $50 million.* Business Insider. https://www.businessinsider.com/blockbuster-ceo-passed-up-chance-to-buy-netflix-for-50-million-2015-7

Civil action. (2018). State of Indiana V Purdue. https://www.in.gov/attorneygeneral/consumer-protection-division/files/2018.11.13-FINAL-State-of-Indiana-v-Purdue-Complaint-Unredacted.pdf

Cunff, A.-L. L. (2022, November 24). *Reopening the mind: How cognitive closure kills creative thinking.* Ness Labs. https://nesslabs.com/cognitive-closure

Forester, B. (2023, May 17). *Toward the data-driven army of 2040: Avoiding analysis paralysis and harnessing the power of Analytics.* Modern War Institute. https://mwi.westpoint.edu/toward-the-data-driven-army-of-2040-avoiding-analysis-paralysis-and-harnessing-the-power-of-analytics/

Gordon, R. (2024, September 30). *AI Pareidolia: Can machines spot faces in inanimate objects?.* MIT News | Massachusetts Institute of Technology. https://news.mit.edu/2024/ai-pareidolia-can-machines-spot-faces-in-inanimate-objects-0930

Harrison, M. (2009, May 11). Soviet managers and accounting fraud, 1943 to 1962. https://warwick.ac.uk/fac/soc/economics/staff/mharrison/public/jce2011postprint.pdf

Heinisch, K., Schult, C., & Stapper, C. (2024). Transparency and forecasting: The impact of conditioning assumptions on forecast accuracy. *Applied Economics Letters*, 1–5. https://doi.org/10.1080/13504851.2024.2388870

Horowitz, J., & Menn, J. (2018, September 19). *Knight trading loss shows cracks in equity markets*. Reuters. https://www.reuters.com/article/business/knight-trading-loss-shows-cracks-in-equity-markets-idUSBRE87203X/

Jerez-Fernandez, A., Angulo, A. N., & Oppenheimer, D. M. (2013). Show me the numbers. *Psychological Science*, *25*(2), 633–635. https://doi.org/10.1177/0956797613504301

Khimm, S., Strickler, L., Blankstein, A., & Georgiev, P. (2020, April 12). *Thousands have died in nursing homes around the U.S. but the federal Gov't isn't tracking them*. NBCNews.com. https://www.nbcnews.com/news/us-news/more-2-200-coronavirus-deaths-nursing-homes-federal-government-isn-n1181026

LeRouge, C., Hasselquist, M. B., Kellogg, L., Austin, E., Fey, B. C., Hartzler, A. L., Flum, D. R., & Lavallee, D. (2017). Using heuristic evaluation to enhance the visual display of a provider dashboard for patient-reported outcomes. *eGEMs (Generating Evidence & Methods to Improve Patient Outcomes)*, *5*(2), 6. https://doi.org/10.13063/2327-9214.1283

Lindgaard, G., Fernandes, G., Dudek, C., & Brown, J. (2006). Attention web designers: You have 50 milliseconds to make a good first impression! *Behaviour & Information Technology*, *25*(2), 115–126. https://doi.org/10.1080/01449290500330448

Mattson, C., Bushardt, R. L., & Artino, A. R. (2021). "When a measure becomes a target, it ceases to be a good measure." *Journal of Graduate Medical Education*, *13*(1), 2–5. https://doi.org/10.4300/jgme-d-20-01492.1

Mazor, M., & Fleming, S. M. (2021). The Dunning-Kruger Effect Revisited. *Nature Human Behaviour*, *5*(6), 677–678. https://doi.org/10.1038/s41562-021-01101-z

Morgan, P. S. (n.d.). *Fault protection techniques in JPL spacecraft*. https://s3vi.ndc.nasa.gov/ssri-kb/static/resources/05-2750.pdf

Nature. (2014). Stap retracted. *Nature*, *511*(7507), 5–6. https://doi.org/10.1038/511005b

Pennestrì, F., Cabitza, F., Picerno, N., & Banfi, G. (2025). Sharing Reliable Information Worldwide: Healthcare strategies based on artificial intelligence need external validation. position paper. *BMC Medical Informatics and Decision Making, 25*(1). https://doi.org/10.1186/s12911-025-02883-2

Richwine, L., & Chmielewski, D. (2024, April 19). *Netflix to stop reporting subscriber tally as streaming wars cool*. Reuters. https://www.reuters.com/technology/netflix-crushes-subscriber-forecasts-second-straight-quarter-2024-04-18/

Rose, T. (2016, January 16). *When U.S. Air Force discovered the flaw of averages.* Toronto Star. https://www.thestar.com/news/insight/when-u-s-air-force-discovered-the-flaw-of-averages/article_e3231734-e5da-5bf5-9496-a34e52d60bd9.html

Salmon, F. (2009, February 23). *Recipe for disaster: The formula that killed Wall Street*. Wired. https://www.wired.com/2009/02/wp-quant/

Sculley, D., Spitznagel, B., Ottey, M., Hainsworth, J., Pohl, M., & Zhou, Y. Y. (2011). *Detecting Adversarial Advertisements in the Wild*. Google. https://static.googleusercontent.com/media/www.google.com/en//pdf/GoogleSearchGuide-back.pdf

SEC. (2023, August 31). *Conditions for use of Non-GAAP financial measures*. U.S. Securities and Exchange Commission. https://www.sec.gov/rules-regulations/2003/03/conditions-use-non-gaap-financial-measures

Select Bipartisan Committee. (2006). *A Failure of Initiative: Final Report.* https://govinfo.library.unt.edu/katrina/levees.pdf

Shepardson, D., & Rucinski, T. (2020, September 13). *Boeing executives defend safety decisions on 737 MAX development*. Reuters. https://www.reuters.com/article/us-boeing-737max-congress/boeing-executives-defend-safety-decisions-on-737-max-development-idUSKBN26404A/

Shepardson, D. (2018, September 19). *U.S. judge dismisses GM ignition switch criminal case*. Reuters. https://www.reuters.com/article/business/us-judge-dismisses-gm-ignition-switch-criminal-case-idUSKCN1LZ2U0/

Singh, K. (2025, January 16). *SEC settles charges against US hedge fund over investment model vulnerabilities*. Reuters. https://www.reuters.com/markets/us/sec-settles-charges-against-us-hedge-fund-over-investment-model-vulnerabilities-2025-01-16/

Statt, N. (2020, July 8). *Quibi reportedly lost 90 percent of early users after their free trials expired*. The Verge. https://www.theverge.com/2020/7/8/21318060/quibi-subscriber-count-free-trial-paying-users-conversion-rate

Time. (1959, November 30). *Autos: The $250 million flop*. https://time.com/archive/6888827/autos-the-250-million-flop

van Veen, V., Krug, M. K., Schooler, J. W., & Carter, C. S. (2009). Neural activity predicts attitude change in cognitive dissonance. *Nature Neuroscience, 12*(11), 1469–1474. https://doi.org/10.1038/nn.2413

Wolford, B. (2024, August 29). *What is GDPR, the EU's new Data Protection Law?* GDPR.eu. https://gdpr.eu/what-is-gdpr/

Xie, G.-X., & Kronrod, A. (2012). Is the devil in the details? *Journal of Advertising, 41*(4), 103–117. https://doi.org/10.1080/00913367.2012.10672460

www.ingramcontent.com/pod-product-compliance
Lightning Source LLC
LaVergne TN
LVHW041704070526
838199LV00045B/1193